Dougie Brimson was born in Hertfordshire in 1959. After school he joined the RAF and spent over eighteen years in the forces before leaving, in 1994, to forge a career as a writer. He co-authored four non-fiction books examining the culture of football hooliganism before moving into fiction with his thriller, *The Crew*. He continues to write both fiction and non-fiction, in addition to his burgeoning career as a television presenter and producer. He is married with three children.

Eddy Brimson was born in 1964. He trained as a graphic designer and set up a successful business before turning to writing in 1995. Over the years he has appeared on television and radio in many different guises, from presenter through to chat-show guest. In May 1999 he set out to pursue his latest passion, stand-up comedy.

'Packed with first-hand accounts of incidents . . . well-paced [and] non-sensationalist' *Mail on Sunday*

'Compelling' *Independent*

'Offers a grim insight into the mind of the football thug' *Daily Mirror*

'Best-selling, ruck-a-page account of football thuggery' *Time Out*

'Honest, funny and refreshingly direct' *Independent on Sunday*

'Exceptionally readable' *Total Football*

'Probably the best book ever written on football violence' *Daily Mail*

DOUGIE & EDDY BRIMSON

EVERYWHERE WE GO

Behind the matchday madness

headline
review

First published in 1996
by HEADLINE BOOK PUBLISHING

This special edition published in 2006
by HEADLINE REVIEW

An imprint of Headline Book Publishing

1

ISBN 0 7553 1519 7

Typeset by Letterpart Limited, Reigate, Surrey

Printed and bound in Great Britain by
Mackays of Chatham plc, Chatham, Kent

Headline's policy is to use papers that are natural, renewable and
recyclable products and made from wood grown in sustainable
forests. The logging and manufacturing processes are expected to
conform to the environmental regulations of the country of origin.

HEADLINE BOOK PUBLISHING
A division of Hodder Headline
338 Euston Road
London NW1 3BH

www.reviewbooks.co.uk
www.hodderheadline.com

Contents

With thanks to Tina for her patience
and the coffee, Mum and Dad,
Ian Marshall for lunch (!),
all those that helped us compile this book
and footy fans everywhere,
except those up the road.

We hate L*t*n
we hate L*t*n
we hate L*t*n
and we hate L*t*n,
we hate L*t*n
and we hate L*t*n
we are the L*t*n haters.

Ev'rywhere we go,
People wanna know
Who the 'ell we are,
So we gotta tell 'em.
We are the Watford,
We play in black and gold
And if you wanna argue,
Come 'n 'ave a go!

Introduction

Many years ago, back in the early seventies, I went to watch Chelsea play at Stamford Bridge. For a thirteen-year-old from Hertfordshire, that was quite a trip because I went alone, drawn by the desire to watch Peter Osgood play, the man who had become an idol of mine even though I had only ever seen him on *The Big Match* or *Match of the Day*.

I had been to games before, of course; the town we live in was full of North London overspill from the Second World War and club allegiances are lifelong. Even today the place is full of armchair Spurs and Gunners fans but we had sworn our loyalty to another club, our local team, Watford FC, and that is where we watched football and grew up in the days before Elton John and Graham Taylor. However, although the Hornets were (and remain) my first love and I was a regular at the Vicarage Road end, I was drawn to Ossie like a moth to a 100 watt bulb. He was a genius, and the memory of the most famous diving header of all time still sends shivers down my spine. I just had to see him play, and it was on my way to this game, at Fulham Broadway tube station to be exact, that something happened which was to have a major influence on my spectating days for many years. A fight broke out. Not just any fight: a full-bore, early-seventies, blue-is-the-colour type semi-riot. I stood rooted to the spot as wave after wave of long-haired, flare-wearing yobs ran past me to beat the living daylights out of those unfortunate opposing supporters who had been in the wrong place at the wrong time. I had read about football violence, of course, and as a schoolboy I had re-enacted various riots with the kids at school (we never saw anything like that at Vicarage Road in those days), but here I was right slap-bang in the middle of one and it was bloody fantastic. I was proud to watch men defending the honour of my hero Ossie's club against some other scum who were attempting to soil their reputation. At least, this was the rosy picture of events I had concocted by the time I arrived home, which was about four o'clock because, as soon as the mob had passed, I was off down the tube and back to Euston like a rocket to get on the first train out of town.

I lived off the back of that story for months, obviously with the deletion of the last part. My programme and train-ticket stub were all I needed to prove that I had been to Chelsea on Saturday and seen a major ruck. The more I told the story, the more I expanded the facts, until, in the end, I got as sick of telling it as other people did of hearing it. But by then I was hooked. Football violence was, for a thirteen-year-old boy, anyway, a very interesting topic of conversation and from that day on I assumed the typical supporter's habit of scanning the crowd at every opportunity, particularly if the visitors scored, for any sign of the enemy within at our end. If we spotted them, we moved as one to where they stood and the pushing and shoving would begin until the police came in and rescued them. Watching football would never be the same again.

I have retained that interest in football violence ever since – not even a lengthy spell in Her Majesty's armed forces, including both the Falklands and the Gulf conflicts, could rid me of the perverse pleasure of reading or hearing accounts of trouble at games and I would be guilty of a major falsehood if I even began to pretend that I had never been involved in incidents at matches, both home and away. My younger brother, with whom this book has been written, has also maintained, shall we say, a presence on the terraces, and although he started somewhat later than I, he has certainly accumulated a far more detailed curriculum vitae than I ever did.

However, this book is not about great we, or Watford FC, are; if it were it would be a work of fiction to rank alongside anything a popular novelist could construct. It is, quite simply, about football violence. We wrote it because on terraces, coaches and trains all over the country, and for countless seasons, we have wanted someone to write it, to stand up and tell people what it is really like to watch from the terraces, but no one did. So, in the end, we had to do it. This book is about who causes violence, why, how and when they do it; about what can be done and by whom to try to stop it and about why, ultimately, it will never be stopped. We have drawn not only on our own experiences, but on information and accounts gathered from interviews and anecdotes sent to us by football supporters all over the country – genuine supporters who are sick to death of reading the pathetic ramblings of pseudo-intellectuals who try to justify their inflated salaries by providing just what the football establishment wants to hear: that we are all working-class, unintelligent, low-skilled products of broken homes. Anything, in short, but the real truth. We have spoken to the victims, the perpetrators, the observers and the establishment during our research and have included transcripts of many of these interviews. In all cases the accounts are reproduced essentially verbatim to give a chilling insight into the way the football supporter can sometimes behave and why.

What we have not done is to produce an A–Z of great football rucks. That would have been an easy route to take, but we wanted to get out there to find and report the real truth. We all know what happened in Galatasaray and with Millwall at Kenilworth Road, and to examine such incidents again would have little real value. Anyone who has ever been involved in the episodes we have dealt with, or anything like them, will acknowledge them as true, but it is certain that those who have only watched and written will dismiss these accounts as at best selective and at worst fiction. We have absolutely no doubt whatsoever that we will get slaughtered for some of the things we have written and that the condemnation will come at us from all sides. However, to use a well-worn phrase, we have been there, seen it, done it, got the T-shirt, and we are confident that what we offer here represents the view of the great majority of football supporters. That is good enough for us. The fact that some of what is written here will be read with disbelief by people within the game serves only to show why things are still as they are.

PART ONE
Everywhere We Go

———————————

Chapter 1
No One Likes Us

Football supporters are a strange breed. I mean, who else would allow themselves to be taken for granted and treated like cattle while paying exorbitant prices for the privilege? These days it is almost fashionable to be a football fan, something trendy to throw into the conversation at parties – Christ, you've even got women playing Fantasy Football on the television and an MP telling us on the radio how 'we' feel about football. Nowadays, watching football is portrayed as a family activity, like going to the pictures or the seaside, although a lot more expensive. This has certainly had a number of major influences on the way the average male supporter behaves inside grounds, because although many male supporters, myself included, believe that if women and children want to go to football they should be given an area to sit in on their own away from the men, there is no doubt that we behave ourselves better if we are in a mixed environment. High-profile policing and closed-circuit television have nothing to do with it. If a woman tells me to shut up I will, and no matter what anyone says, you cannot comfortably let forth a stream of Anglo-Saxon expletives if there's an eight-year-old sitting behind you. This, together with the loss of terracing, has led to the disappearance of the male-only environment we grew up in and fell in love with.

EVERYWHERE WE GO

When I started going to football, women seemed to be outlawed anyway – I honestly cannot remember ever seeing any women at matches – and so the male characteristics of swearing, lying, drinking and fighting were not only prevalent, they were almost compulsory. To be among thousands of young men, all of whom, for those ninety minutes at least, had just one focus in life, was to be part of what the Americans would call a huge male-bonding process. It mattered not that we were schoolboys, mechanics, businessmen, shopkeepers, rich or poor, because for those ninety minutes we were all football supporters and that was all we were. The defence of our club through shouting, cheering and fighting was all we had in mind; that was what we did and that was what thousands of other people did all over the country on every matchday.

The sociologists and anthropologists would have you believe that football hooligans originated from a specific background, the working classes and broken homes, and were simply acting out our rituals and tribal traditions. When Margaret Thatcher had been in power for long enough, she got the blame for us as well, because we came from the underclass she was busy expanding. Everything they said about us, the media and the football establishment lapped up (and still trot out every time there is a major incident at a game), because these theories were shifting the blame, and therefore the responsibility, away from football, which was precisely what everybody was desperate for. But these theories have one fatal flaw: they are total bollocks. Everyone on the terraces has known that for years and has laughed long and hard at them.

What the 'intellectuals' failed to realise, or did not want to accept, was that the people who take part in football violence came, and come, from all walks of life and look upon football as being 'theirs', their escape from the everyday pressures of work or home. The rubbish the 'experts' spouted actually helped many of us who did not fit what was considered to be the standard hooligan profile. If caught, we pleaded innocence, and more often than not we got away with it because people like us could not possibly have been involved, could we? (As an ex-serviceman, I can state from experience that a military identity card is as good as any solicitor when negotiating your release from the cells.) During my time I have known many highly paid and highly skilled professional people who have been actively involved in both the organisation and the execution of football violence, and they are not isolated cases but large numbers of people. These days it is rare indeed to meet anyone unemployed at football because the cost of admission is too high, especially since the clubs have stopped many of the concessions that used to be so popular when ground capacities were larger and crowds smaller.

So the old chestnut of social deprivation does not hold water and never has, but there is another theory which is even wider of the mark than this, one which is still regularly trotted out for the media but could not be further from the truth. It is the assumption that football fans cause trouble to express their discontent at the loss of their game to big business and the executive-box movement. How patronising can you possibly get? Do these people honestly believe that every time something happens at football it is because supporters actually want to disrupt the growth of their own club by soiling its good name and thereby damaging any future investment in it? Where do they get this stuff from? The sad thing is that if they ever bothered to ask the people involved in football violence why they do it, they would get the same answer over and over again. People fight because people like to fight. Football is the vehicle they use because they can justify violence as the defence of their team, town or reputation. They see their role as an extension of that of their teams: to beat the opposition. Through the media both clubs and the establishment claim that the perpetrators of violence are not fans of football but purely fans of violence. Yet these are the very people who travel the country and sit or stand in the wind and rain to support their team on a level that chairman and directors cannot possibly understand. It is a love of their club taken to a different and higher plane, and that really is all there is to it. Football violence is like smoking, if you try it once and hate it, you don't do it again, but if you try it once and like it, it's bloody hard to give it up.

To ask people why they indulge in violence of this kind is really to ask a pointless question. If you ask a gambler why he gambles or a drinker why he drinks, you will get the same reply: he likes doing it. People who fight are no different, and if they fight among themselves or indulge in their 'interest' with other like-minded individuals (which they do 90 per cent of the time anyway) no one would care less. People fight outside pubs and clubs every Saturday night and we don't see it as a major issue, but if they do it at football matches we are incensed, and quite rightly so, because at football, especially inside stadiums, innocent bystanders can sometimes become involved and that's where the problems start. However, as someone with an interest, albeit an inactive one now, I have no problem understanding why people defend their clubs in such an extreme manner. For others it is a reasoning that must be explored (although before you become too self-righteous, can you honestly say that you have never seen people from your club fighting and actively urged them on to victory? For that moment at least, you understood why).

To begin this process you need to ask one simple question: 'Why do you like football?' Of course, you can go into the old, it's-a-wonderful-game, emotional-rollercoaster sort of thing, but for the average male devotee football is much more than that: it is bound into his life because it is part of the move from youth to manhood. The often-repeated words, 'I grew up on those/these terraces' tell it all, because, as young men everywhere will realise at some stage, going to football was probably the first time they really went out on their own. That is an important stage in anyone's life, when you quickly realise that you can escape the clutches of your parents every week and can do anything without their knowledge (my parents still believe that we never got up to anything at football). How many young men had their first cigarette, their first drink, shouted their first swearword or had their first fight at a football match? Significant points in a young man's life and, some would argue, important parts of growing up. You meet your mates, have a laugh, get to scream your head off and escape into a world which belongs only to you, never mind the rest of the crowd, and you experience every emotion possible within the ninety minutes of a game. It gets to be a drug; you cannot give it up and the matchdays cannot come fast enough. The obsession begins and takes you over to such a degree that planning your life around the fixture list becomes normal and entirely reasonable behaviour. When you arrive at this stage of your obsession, a number of things can happen. You can either stay where you are, acknowledge your state of mind and stop, or you can try to increase the dose by becoming even more involved in some way.

It should be noted here that we are talking about men, not women, because women do not fight at football (Lincoln and Newport County excepted) and I believe that there is a simple reason for this. Women like football. They don't love or worship it, they *like* it, and that's the difference. All men know that if things had been only slightly different, they could have been out there alongside Wright and Shearer at St James's Park or Wembley. That's why we get so passionate about what the players are doing. Women cannot do that because they can never actually play football at the highest levels like men and therefore they cannot possibly become as involved in the game with the same passion. For them, any game is just an event, but for men it's a dream of what could, and damn it, should have been.

So there you are, a committed fan but desperate for more; the usual Saturday fix is no longer enough. The next phase is to become involved with the main body of supporters at 'the End', be it the Kop, North Stand or whatever. This family of supporters, always on the lookout for new members, will, after a reasonable period, accept you as one of their own and now you really do belong, you're part of 'the Mob'. When you get involved with the mob environment that quickly forms when a few like-minded individuals come together, things take on a different perspective because, as mentioned earlier, you perceive yourselves to be on a plane above the average supporter.

It is your role to defend your team's honour and reputation as well as your own, and it is to you that the normal fan will call when the opposing fans begin trouble. You now have a personal importance; the performance of the team becomes almost secondary at times. What matters is that you out-sing the visiting fans or, if any are brave enough to come into your end, that 'the Mob', which includes you, fight them and beat them. That's your victory, you did it, and the buzz you feel from conflict, and ultimately victory, is so real you can almost touch it. The basic instinct in all young men is to prove their courage, not only to others but to themselves, and for many, football offers the only viable arena in which to do it.

Sooner or later, though, a time will come when you are faced with a situation which will entail you actually hitting someone or getting hit, and that's when things start to get confused. I have seen people become involved in fights at football who were physically sick afterwards and were never seen at games again, and I can well understand that reaction. Violence is a horrific thing, it's not the sanitised item that television delivers to our screens. Getting hit bloody well hurts, and the realisation of this is significant. There is one thing I would be very interested to know but which would be impossible to find out, and that is how many people who have been actively involved in football violence were actually on the losing side the first time they experienced it. I don't mean getting run or anything so simple, I mean taking a good hiding. I bet it's not that many. In football defeat hurts, but nowhere near as much as a kick in the groin.

Another important factor to consider is that people who carry out these acts do not really see violence at football as a criminal act, and while the majority of them would never dream of walking up to someone and attacking them during their everyday lives, at a game they will do it readily and, if caught, struggle to understand the problem. So there you are, involved and part of the mob; you've proved yourself at some time and people know that you will stand and not do a runner if it goes off. Now, although still obsessed with your club, you perceive your own performance to be as important as that of the team. When at home you defend (your reputation) and when away you attack (their reputation). However, as touched on earlier, what is often overlooked is that the hooligan is passionate about his team in a way that no player or manager could ever be. To a player or manager the club is just another job, and if he is transferred, then he switches his allegiance at the stroke of a pen on a contract. (There are obvious exceptions to this rule. Tony Adams and Steve Bull are two that spring to mind, but every club has them.) For supporters things are different. The bond is lifelong, they are part of their club and their club is part of them. They can spend the whole match screaming abuse at their own players but if a visiting fan utters a single word he is dead meat. He has no right to criticise, and what he says become a personal insult to be treated accordingly.

Another factor relating to mob violence at games is the phenomenon of 'like mind', when an individual loses control of his own actions and becomes embroiled in violence as a result. The poll-tax riots in the eighties provided a classic example of this. People were just sucked into the violence and did things they would otherwise never have even considered doing. My father, a Spurs fan, once told me about watching a game many years ago which had become pretty fierce. The Spurs crowd was already fairly well roused when the opposing full-back hacked down one of the Tottenham players. The supporters were incensed, screaming like animals for this thug to be sent off, my old man included. But then he dropped his cigarette and bent down to pick it up, narrowly missing getting his head trodden on in the process. In the few seconds it took him to retrieve the cigarette and avoid injury, the mental link between himself and the rest of the crowd was broken. When he stood up, he found himself in the midst of a horde of baying animals. He said it was a terrifying experience, standing alone in the middle of a hostile crowd and feeling the hate and potential for violence as if it were tangible. This mass hysteria manifests itself in other ways, of course, and I have found myself steaming down a road, across a terrace or even away from a mob before I actually knew what I was doing, as if I sensed what was happening before I could see it.

Of course, as supporters get older, things change. The pressures of modern life and the way football has started to get its act together in its dealings with the public make it very different now from when I was eighteen. Football doesn't exert the same draw on young men as it used to – there are far too many other forms of entertainment available to an active youth with an increased capacity for travel. The mob culture that was highly vocal at football grounds is now being replaced by a different, family-friendly environment, which is unquestionably a good thing. Yet if anyone thinks for one moment that the problem of football violence has vanished – well, I'm sorry, you can think again. There may be only the odd row inside grounds, usually quite brief and involving a few idiots who should know better, but the obsessive behaviour of the mob has not moved far and it is still fiercely allied to football. At the moment it is unfashionable to fight on a large scale inside stadiums, but this trend has merely moved the problem outside into the surrounding areas, and this in turn has made the fighting a far more brutal and savage affair. The young men who perpetrated acts of violence on the terraces of clubs during the seventies and eighties have been supplemented by a new breed, forced by the changes within the game and assisted by increased wealth and technology to become more organised. They may fight in a different environment and even in a different way, but what they do, who they are and the reasons why they do it remain the same.

At this point we need to examine a question that is often trotted out in discussions about football hooligans, and that is 'Why football and not rugby?' Christ, how often have you heard that old chestnut after a high-profile off at a game? Exactly, every bloody time – and if you're like me, it gets right on your tits, so before we progress further we need to examine this issue and get it over with once and for all. Many boys played rugby at school; for some perverse reason some schools actually prefer it to football, which usually has something to do with the sports teacher and his university background. Having said that, personally, I actually became quite good at rugby at school and even enjoyed forays back to the game for the odd sevens tournament during my time in the forces. Like most Englishmen, I relish the success of our national rugby team while wishing that 'our' team were half as good, but like most football supporters, I would swap the England rugby team winning the World Cup for a single Watford win, any Watford win (substitute your own team here – I realise that not all of you will share our hopes). If such a choice were offered to me, there would be no hesitation whatsoever, because in truth I don't give a toss about rugby, for one simple reason: it's not *my* game. I can only really remember one rugby match I ever played in and that is because I got badly hurt, but I can remember loads of footy games, and that is the essential difference between the two sports as far as I am concerned. As a kid, I didn't play rugby after school or at weekends, I played football. I could go out with my trusty orange plastic ball and play on my own for hours and, even if no one else turned up, I could practise bending free kicks or play 'keep up' for hours. You just can't play tennis, rugby or cricket on your own, football was easy, that's why it's my game. The same thing can be said by almost every football supporter in Britain. How many people do you know who even own a rugby ball? How many people do you know who get up on Sunday mornings and go out to play rugby for their pub side? How many top-flight rugby clubs can you even name, never mind tell me where they play? We rest our case.

The great beauty of football is that anyone can play, at any time and in any place; indeed, it was in those mass games involving loads of kids (and the odd dad) with jumpers for goals that we became our heroes and fell in love with the great game and everything it could give us, including the heartbreak and the elation. The people who watch rugby will be saying 'Well, you try to get a ticket for an international game and then tell me it isn't popular.' Fine, I'm not saying it isn't popular, but you look at those sell-out crowds at Twickenham and tell me how many of those who are there courtesy of some corporate empire will be out watching their local side at the weekend or throwing a ball around with their kids? Much the same thing can be said about cricket. Again, the international games are sell-outs, but how many of your average blokes actually play it, unless they're messing around on a beach? Football is different. I defy anyone not to feel a touch of nostalgia when they look at those old photographs of East End urchins kicking a ball about on a cobbled street. Don't the memories come flooding back when you see those old recordings of games long past? Great games in which we, yes, you or me, did things that would make Jimmy Greaves or even Romario gasp in wonder. Vivid recollections of fearsome headers, 40-yard netbusters, sendings-off and crunching tackles; memories that will live with us forever to be reviewed through rose-coloured glasses in quiet moments when life is crap and we need a boost.

For those of us no longer playing, either through age, physical ineptitude, laziness or a mixture of all three, these memories assume secondary importance to those matches we have witnessed in which our boys have got everything just right and gone to town on crap opposition (or, even better, our local rivals) or have scrapped or scraped a win out of nothing. The 2–1 wins at Old Trafford, the 8–0 thrashing of Sunderland, these are the games of which dreams are made, the games that make the long journeys and soaking wet terraces worthwhile. We know that every match we go to see could possibly become one of these, and you don't get them in any other sport like you do in football because – and I don't care what anyone says – no sport means as much to its fans as football does to us. That's why we go, and why we are so completely enthralled by football, and that, simply, is why you sometimes get trouble at football and not at rugby.

Chapter 2
The Way In

This chapter is an account, sent to us anonymously, which explains how a supporter became involved in violence. His life is, we believe, typical of many others. We reproduce it in full in order to show how one man's participation in hooliganism can evolve, and what it is that motivates him.

This is the story is how I became involved as a member of one of the most respected firms in the country and how, basically, I became addicted to football violence.

I come from a small Home Counties town, have a managerial job and live with my girlfriend and our two children. My father was a professional gentleman who ran his own business and I was brought up in a beautiful house with my younger sister and never really wanted for anything. I led a sheltered life away from the gang warfare of the local council estates, which was big news around our town at the time, so I was not a 'face' and could, if I wanted to, travel to any part of the town without any hint of trouble.

Since I was eleven, my father and an uncle had taken me on occasions to watch Watford, our local team, and I loved it. But they only took me about five times a year and I began longing for more. One Saturday, when I was about fourteen, I did what most boys end up doing and went to

Vicarage Road on my own without telling my mum where I was going. The thrill of that day is still with me – the thought that I might get seen and that my parents would find out made it all the more exciting, and when I got home afterwards, no one even asked where I had been. I had got away with it.

This started to become a regular thing as I attended almost every home game while my mum, happy that I was building a social life for myself, sometimes wondered why she never met any of my new friends. After about six or seven matches, I started to recognise some of the faces on the way to the game and one day one of the other lads of about my age came over and asked me if I was going to the match. When I said I was, he asked if I wanted to go with them as they all lived in my town and went up every week. That felt fantastic. I was no longer on my own but going to the game as part of a group of lads. Little did I know it, but these lads were to change my life.

When we got to the ground, we went to the opposite end from where I usually stood, and for the first time I found myself standing quite near to the visiting supporters. I will never forget that feeling in my stomach, looking across at about 150 Newport County supporters who were doing their utmost to out-sing us. The lads I was with seemed to know everyone around us and introduced me to loads of people, and I really began to feel a part of something. It was quite an amazing feeling for a fourteen-year-old. The atmosphere was different from anything I had ever experienced – everyone was singing and shouting and when we scored, it wasn't the refined applause I was used to with my father and uncle, it was total chaos, absolutely brilliant!

At half-time, one of the lads told me they were going over to stand near the away fans and wind them up a bit for the older lads. He explained that this happened at every home game. Towards the end of the match, the older lads would drift over one by one, and once they had sufficient numbers in that part of the ground they would probably attack. I could not believe what I was hearing, there seemed to be no sense at all to it. I mean, why? was the obvious question. I had never been in a fight in my life.

I have looked back on this moment many times because it was a major turning point in my life. I have often wondered what would have happened to me had I not gone with them, but I was with a group of lads who had invited me into their little circle and there was no way I was going to look soft in front of them, so I followed. I remember thinking that, close up, Newport County fans were huge and quickly realised that any one of them could do me permanent damage, but the other lads were hurling abuse at them and they were getting very aggressive. I was getting very close to the point where I was about to run when the cry went up and I realised that all of the older lads had made their way over. Suddenly, all hell broke loose as people ran in every direction. Within seconds, the police appeared out of nowhere and I soon realised that we were standing in the spot the Newport fans had occupied only minutes before and they were standing down in the corner by the tea bar. The police rounded us all up and moved us back to our original place while the rest of the crowd cheered as if we had won a great victory. As our group moved back, all the older lads patted us on the back for our part in their victory. We were part of it all. What a feeling!

The same thing happened over and over again at home games. We never got turned over and I never received anything more than the odd shove, but things took a very different turn at my first away game, which happened to be a midweek match at Brentford. There was always trouble at our place when we played them, and it was well known that this continued at their place, but the chance actually to go there and take them on was too good to miss. In those days, the silk scarf was the height of fashion and my friends and I had ours hanging round our necks to let everyone know who we were, something we quickly realised was not such a good idea as we were well and truly outnumbered and were on our own. We turned into a road and found a load of the older lads drinking outside a pub. Suddenly we felt more confident and a lot safer. This was more like it.

They were all on good form after a few beers and we began talking about Brentford supporters and past trouble with them when someone told us that they had heard that a mob from Chelsea were supposed to be coming up to fight with the Brentford mob, but that they had bottled it. This was a standard rumour in those days, and even I didn't really believe it. But as we left the lads and made our way up the road we heard an almighty noise. When we turned, we saw the pub being attacked with bottles and bricks and our lot getting a bit of a hiding and being run up the road towards us. I could hear the odd shout of 'Chelsea!' and ran for my life. This was a different game altogether. I could get hurt and I was scared.

Once we made it into the game, the atmosphere was very different from our place, much more intense, but our mob was much bigger than the usual one, which was probably something to do with us all being in the same part of the ground. All through the game we were attacking their fans and then they would run at us. I remember seeing one of our lads being taken out with blood streaming down his face after being hit – with a brick, I think – but as the St Johns led him round the pitch, he turned and ran at the Brentford mob and dived in on his own. When he came back out, he just walked across the pitch and waved at us. What a hero!

When the game finished, all the Brentford supporters from the other end came streaming across the pitch towards us, but someone was shouting at us all to get up the back to the exits. As the first Brentford supporters came over the wall, a shout went up and all our lot turned and steamed down at them. Those they caught took a right hiding while the rest just ran – it was an amazing thing to see. As we left the ground we were so excited. We turned a corner to find a huge mob of Brentford coming up the road from the side stand. These were the people we had been fighting during the game. My scarf was off and down my trousers in a flash and I quickly ducked down behind a car. Once again the roar went up and the Brentford mob came running past; then we saw the familiar faces chasing up the road after them. We were now running them. The scarves were out and off we went, running with the mob, not knowing where we were going or why, but what a buzz. The police finally caught up with us and after a while escorted us back to the tube station and away. We had been in another town and had been taking liberties: the feeling of power was incredible – we could have taken anyone that night. I was hooked.

Later that season we drew West Ham in the FA Cup down at Upton Park, and we knew that this would be the biggest test we had ever faced. This was the big time we had all wanted, but deep down we all knew that they would waste no time in trying to put us firmly in our place. Make no bones about it, that game was scary, mostly because we made the mistake of travelling by tube and were well and truly sussed out long before we arrived in East London. The walk down the road to the ground was one of the most scary moments of my life. I saw a chip-shop window that had been put through and this bloke came up to me and told me that they had just thrown a Watford fan through it, and that he would be looking for me after the game as there were loads of other windows to aim at. At that point I would rather have slept on the terrace for the night than leave the ground and walk back down the road at full-time.

During the game it was going off all the time, and to be honest, we did all right. At the end we felt that if anything our reputation had been boosted because we had gone to West Ham in good numbers and we had a go back.

Away games became the focus for us. Pitch invasions at Torquay, Scunthorpe and Bournemouth; taking the home ends at Northampton and Crewe, where the wall collapsed and the match was held up for twenty minutes – all of these helped us to gain the reputation we were after. Promotion in that season meant that there were new challenges and we continued to travel and take people on whenever we could. Going to Old Trafford and beating them 2–1 in the League Cup and then getting mobbed up and taking the piss out of the 'Mancs" all the way to the station was for me one of the highlights of the season. Taking a mob of 400 up to Carlisle for a night game and setting fire to the programme stall was another, but we also came up against some bigger firms, such as Blackpool, who were more than up for it, and Plymouth.

The real turning point for us as a mob was the trip to Sheffield Wednesday. This was a big match – it was near the end of the season and we were both up for promotion, and it was estimated that we would be taking about 6,000 supporters. We knew full well that Wednesday would give us a reception to remember. As we entered Sheffield, we saw loads of Watford supporters heading back to the motorway. We stopped at some lights and this guy opposite us got out of his car and came over to us. He told us that he was a Watford fan and that the Sheffield supporters had been turning cars over, the club coaches had been wrecked and more of their fans were running riot and throwing small steel bars at anyone they suspected of being a Watford fan. We had travelled in a small convoy of minibuses with some other people from our town, and as some of them had never been involved in any trouble, we pulled over to decide what to do. It was decided that one bus would turn straight round and anyone who wanted to could just leave while the rest of us would go to the game, but would wait where we were until the last possible moment. When we got to the ground, there couldn't have been more than 700 of our lot there. We felt gutted – our reputation had been completely shattered in just one game. I remember seeing the coaches as we left the ground and they had been well and truly hit. We had been turned over big-time.

That summer, I was to get my revenge on Wednesday. Myself and a friend who had been at that game went on holiday to Great Yarmouth and one night we were in this nightclub called Tiffany's. Also inside this club was a large group of West Ham supporters and a group of Wednesday fans. When we left the club, the West Ham lads had mobbed up outside. Once they realised that we were southern football fans they asked us if we wanted to help them out because they were about to turn over the Wednesday lot. Lovely. When the Wednesday supporters came out, they walked straight through the West Ham mob and we started to follow them. But when we got to the street corner, they turned and ran straight back at us. The West Ham lot were off like a rocket, leaving the two of us facing about twenty Yorkshiremen intent on beating the shit out of us. Now, there was no way I was going to take a hiding on the pretence of being a West Ham fan, so we also did the off, but the problem was that the Wednesday fans seemed more interested in the two of us than they did in the rest of them. I remember this big, fat northern bloke chasing up the road after me long after the others had given up. I was giving him loads of verbal while running just fast enough to be out of reach until he nearly had a heart attack and had to stop.

My friend and I were well and truly pissed off with this West Ham lot and decided that we would put on a show for the Watford. When we found the Wednesday mob, they had got back together and were on a roundabout making loads of noise. We quickly went through every garden we could find and collected about a dozen milk bottles and lined them up. We shouted down the road to them and started singing 'The Watford'. When they saw us, they came steaming up the road after us. When they got close enough, we let fly with the bottles and they went in every direction, although one got a direct hit and put this bloke flat on his arse. It was now time to leave, but we felt we had paid them back a little for the hiding they had dished out to us earlier that season.

By now, our club was doing all it could to drive us out. The ground had become much better segregated and the chances to get at the away fans were almost zero. After the Sheffield incident, many of the lads had dropped out of the group and although we were still having the odd big one, it wasn't at the same level as before. I wanted more action, and so I began to follow the England team.

Going to Wembley was a real eye-opener. The first match I attended was in 1979 against Bulgaria in the build-up to the European Championships to be held in Italy the following year. I remember walking around Wembley thinking that this was the biggest mob I had ever seen in my life (there weren't that many Bulgarians!), and the feeling of being proud to be English overwhelmed me. England qualified for the finals and some friends and I decided to take our first holiday abroad in Italy to follow the national side. Everybody was fully aware of the English reputation, but for me this only added to the excitement. We were going to Italy with the intention of giving them a good hiding in their own country.

When we arrived, we stayed on one of the campsites that the Italians had provided, which was right next to a bridge. Every night the locals threw bricks and bottles down on to us. As the police seemed determined to do nothing about it, the English fans were well and truly worked up by the time we went off to Turin for the first game. At the match the police gave us constant grief, along with the locals, who continually threw missiles at us. When the police moved in to take someone out, we had had enough and started to fight back, hitting out at anything that wasn't English. The police steamed back in and when they failed to gain control, they fired tear gas at us, which was really a bit over the top. But what struck me above all else was that the English supporters stood firm and fought it out as best they could. We were immediately branded as scum all over Europe, but of course no one was interested in the treatment we had been receiving, which was the main reason why it had gone off in the first place. All they were interested in was that we were animals. During the next few days, we started to knock about with some of the other groups of supporters on the site, mainly for safety reasons, and among those was a mob from one of the bigger London clubs, a group I was to meet up with again a few years later.

Later in the tournament we had to play the Italians, and you can imagine the hostility that had built up against us. Many of the English supporters decided to return home or move to another part of Italy and watch it on television. Along with some of the other lads, we decided to brave it, because this was an experience we would never forget and we didn't want to be seen to have bottled out. That game was frightening. Getting to the ground was a nightmare and rumours of stabbings were flying around, while the police were busy making it obvious that they were not there to help us out in any way at all. One of our lot was attacked on the way to the stadium because we were waving a huge Union Jack fixed to a wooden pole. This mob of Italians surrounded him and were trying to steal it, but he ripped it off the pole and stuffed it as best he could up his shirt and started to run. This mob grabbed the pole and went after him, one of them catching him across the back of the head. He went down but luckily managed to get up and away. The police didn't give a shit, despite the blood pouring down his face, and just pushed him, and us, into the ground as fast as they could.

During the game we were pissed on, spat on and had firecrackers thrown down on us, but the most frightening thing was when someone threw a small petrol bomb into the area where we were standing. Thankfully, not many English fans had turned up and we had room to move away from the flames, because if the terrace had been full, a great many people could have got badly burned. Italy won the game, which seemed to calm things down a bit, and the police finally gave us some protection but England were out of the competition and we decided to return home early. I still felt proud of myself for putting up a show, but the whole experience changed my way of thinking. If we were going to be treated like scum whenever we travelled abroad, we would behave like scum, and anyone who came to Wembley would be fair game, no matter where they came from. That view was shared by everyone who endured that trip.

Over the next couple of seasons, I continued to fight for Watford. We were on the up and support was growing, and those who had left the mob were being replaced by new blood. Promotion was firing people up again and it meant more derby games against London clubs. We had some great battles at QPR and Crystal Palace as well as at Norwich and Cardiff, but the one that sticks in my mind is Derby County on the last day of the season. We were already promoted and the First Division loomed for the first time in our history. Derby needed to win to stay up, and at a ground renowned for its atmosphere anyway, you can imagine what it was like. We had one of the biggest mobs I'd ever seen us take anywhere that day, and we were going for it big time – opening the perimeter gates in an attempt to get on the pitch, the full works. The police were really pissed off with us and kicked the gravel from around the pitch into our faces and hit out with their truncheons whenever we got up on the fences. As it happened, Derby won the game and at the end invaded the pitch and came across to give us the biggie. We finally managed to get one of the gates open, about a hundred Watford managed to get on the pitch and Derby did a runner.

Outside we ran them everywhere. The police sent the horses in to sort us out and charged us down the alley that runs behind the end. Even though it was packed, the horses still came through and the police were hitting out at anyone. One guy got trampled on and was badly hurt and, as you can imagine, we were starting to get really pissed off. Something made one of the horses rear up and a copper got pulled off. He had his foot or something caught in the stirrups and the horse started to drag him along as it tried to get out. He took probably the worst kicking I have ever seen anyone take in my life. The poor bastard had blood coming out of his eyes.

Since the battles in Italy, I had kept in touch with many of the lads I had met there. We had even been to an England game together, and they kept asking me to go to a League match with them to see a real firm in action. Club loyalties forced me to decline their offer, but promotion meant that we would indeed meet on the terraces – only this time we would be on opposing sides. We knew they would come to our place and put on a show. It was one of those fixtures you dream about at a small club but dread when it arrives, and my mates kept ringing me up and taking the piss, telling me what they were going to do to our place and everything else that went with it, including me. Come the big day, they took over the town and I remember thinking that it must be so fantastic to support a club with a following that big. They were in every pub and every street, and the Watford fans were nowhere to be seen – though in our case it was because we had decided to split up and get to the ground, where we would form up inside to repel the attack on our end that we knew would come.

When I got inside, it was clear that most people had been thinking along the same lines – we had gathered quite a decent mob together. We waited by the turnstiles to spot them as they came in and there were plenty of them to see, including some familiar faces. It was obvious that they were going for it in a big way. There was no way we could let them walk all over us like this, and when one of them spotted me, I decided to make a stand before they were all inside. I went for this bloke while the rest of my group saw me go and followed. The police were over in a flash and got them away and into a corner, from where they were led out. I looked across at my mate and waved goodbye to him as he made his exit. He was not best pleased, but when I rang him the next day we were creasing up about it all; it was respect all round. During the game, the rest of their lot who had managed to make it in kicked everything off, but they were expecting to have bigger numbers and were surprised at the size of the mob we had ready for them, so things ended up pretty even on the day.

I continued to hook up with these lads at England games and eventually took them up on their offer of an away League trip. I had always wondered what it would be like [running with a top firm] and there was only one way to find out. It was an eye-opener. We travelled up by train and stopped at the first pub we came to. By 11.30 we were beginning a serious session; by one o'clock, the place was packed with blokes who had formed into a serious mob. The time had come for them to introduce themselves to the locals and let them know we had arrived. The feeling was fantastic – this was more like it. It had been a long time since Watford had gone on the offensive at an away game (other than at derbies and the Derby match), and it was interesting to see things from a different perspective – there but not involved, if you understand what I mean. The police were on us immediately, but it didn't really matter to anyone. We just went where we wanted and they just shadowed. As we made our way through the town, we could see the local firm up ahead. They started to give us loads of verbal and threw the odd milk bottle while the police just blocked our way and stopped us moving.

It was just like the old days, only better, and I could appreciate what was happening much more now than I had before. The police thought they had it sussed, but some of our lot had slipped round them and let out the signal for us to run at them. Before they realised what was happening most of the group had got past them and were up the road after their firm. After a minor ruck, the police managed to get everyone else rounded up and herded us to the ground and inside. Although the match went off without trouble, the day wasn't over for this lot. There had been talk all day of stopping off at a mainline station on the way back and ambushing the Leeds fans – Leeds had been playing in London that day. Everyone seemed up for it. It was all new to me and really got me buzzing.

When we arrived at the station, we all got off and made our way to the buffet and waiting rooms. If the Leeds fans had a special coming out of London at the usual time, it would stop here in about thirty minutes' time. We sat and waited while some of the others went to get themselves tooled up. In all there must have been about 150 of us waiting for them. When it came, the noise was deafening: we just let fly with everything we had. We could see that some of the Leeds supporters were getting off and coming for us, but most of them didn't have a clue what was going on and were shitting it. We steamed up the stairs to meet them on the bridge but they turned and ran because we had them well outnumbered. We followed them across the bridge, picking the odd one off, but not down on to the platform because there we would have been outnumbered ourselves. The train pulled out quite quickly after that and, luckily for them, they all managed to get on board before it went. After about ten minutes the police turned up in force, gathered us together and got us on the first train back to London without arresting anyone. What a great day, and a great introduction to running with a top firm.

Over the next few seasons I ran with that firm more and more, particularly at the games where we knew the opposition had a serious reputation. I still went to Watford, but the buzz of going on the offensive had got hold of me and it wasn't really the same any more. By the start of the 1989–90 season, I was more committed to this firm than any other, including the Hornets. They soon introduced me to members of one of the top Scottish firms and we went north of the border several times for big derby and grudge matches.

Much of the connection with the Scottish clubs is political, and our firm do have a number of members with right-wing beliefs. But for me the politics don't come into it: I go for the 'offs', pure and simple. Many of the lads from our firm go to England games and get accused of being racist and all that stuff, but to me that's not correct. Personally, I consider myself to be nationalistic and will fight to defend our flag – that stems from the Italian experience – but I won't boo black players or refuse to cheer when a black player scores, the 'black goals don't count' mentality. There are still a few racists about, although there are fewer and fewer these days, thankfully.

In the last couple of seasons, we have continued to be active and have fought all over the country on our travels. We've also planned some great hits – one in particular on a pub in oxford where one of our lot had a pitchfork stuck up his arse – but it has not always gone to plan. We had planned to do a return visit to Leeds to turn one of their pubs over, but we were followed, and when we turned up, they were ready and waiting for us. Fair play to them, though, they had us well and truly sussed, but I'm sure we'll meet again.

During this last season, it has become clear to me, and the rest of us, that the violence is beginning to creep back into the game on a wider scale, but, as a member of one of the worst firms around, I can't really say I'm sorry, can I? The English clubs abroad and events in Dublin are testament to this, while the threat of CCTV has worn off and all-seater stadiums never had any effect anyway. Over the years our club (I still feel uncomfortable saying that) has tried everything to get rid of the hooligan element, but it just will not work because there are thousands of people like me who just live for that buzz. The feeling you get when you're out with a load of blokes and actively looking for trouble is what keeps it all going. And it's not just at football: go down the tube on any Saturday and you'll see it. I've even been to a rock concert for a pre-arranged 'meeting' with two other firms. The game won't stop us, it has to accept that; it may make things difficult for a while, but we'll just change our tactics, which will make it easier to hit other mobs until they catch up with what we are doing. Trust me, we're here to stay until we decide to give it up on our own – and, personally, I can't see that happening for a good while yet.

PART TWO
Why? Because!

Chapter 3
Derby Days

If there is one thing which has the capacity to change even the most mild-mannered supporter into a screaming demon, it is a local derby. The distance matters not one iota; geographical circumstances might dictate that your nearest rival club is over an hour away, but when you meet in a competitive situation, it's local. We have lost count of the number of times during almost every season that we've heard, and indeed spoken, the immortal words: 'I don't care what happens as long as we beat those bastards!' For the average supporter riding the emotional rollercoaster that is football, the local derby is the loop-the-loop, the bit we can't wait for but which we secretly hate because it holds the most fear. Of course, there are those in football who will have you believe that there are only really a small number of true local derby matches – the Merseyside and Manchester games, any combination of Tottenham, Arsenal, West Ham or Chelsea (not QPR or Palace: there's no real history or passion there, and these clubs have always been considered far too trendy, anyway), the Sheffield and Newcastle games (when United or Sunderland are in the top division), and, of course, the Old Firm match.

The astute among you will have noticed a few omissions from that list, and that is because outside Glasgow and the Premier League, local games are looked upon as quaint contests full of regional good humour but lacking any real commitment or importance. Now, on the terraces of these clubs, battling to get into the very top flight which views us with such disdain, we know that this is not the case at all. Try telling the supporters of Bristol Rovers that their match against City is merely another game and they will laugh in your face, because to them, and the fans of, for example, Cardiff and Swansea or Cambridge and Peterborough, those games are the most important of the year. There is real hatred between opposing fans at local derbies, hatred that is often carried over into everyday life, and if you have any doubt as to just how serious these rivalries are taken, think back to the merger of Oxford and Reading which was proposed during the Maxwell era. What, on paper at least, was actually quite a sensible idea managed to stir up some of the most intense debate and protest ever seen in football and eventually the plan was scrapped which, if nothing else, proved that Mr Maxwell had as little understanding of football supporters' loyalty as it was possible to have. A typical chairman, in fact.

Of course, we have a vested interest here because at Watford we have our own local rivals, a team referred to by everyone at the club as 'Shit Town' or 'the Scum', and that team is L*t*n Town. Having watched the Hornets for many years, we can only assume that every supporter in the land feels the same as we do about their own local rivals (and conversations with people all over the country have confirmed that they do indeed). We hate with a passion anything to do with L*t*n, the sight of their kit on a fan's back (thankfully rare in our town), the thought of their horrendously awful ground with its allotment-type sheds along one side and any mention of their players or overrated manager (whoever he is, he is overrated). The sad individuals who support them we view with disgust, because if watching the Scum play is the highlight of their week, then they must be devastatingly pathetic people indeed. We positively refuse to go into sports shops which stock their kit (fortunately few and far between anyway) and would never dream of owning a

Vauxhall (manufactured by their former, misguided sponsors) in a million years. Tradesmen who arrive at our homes are quizzed as to their allegiances and *Fever Pitch*, the excellent Nick Hornby book, lies unfinished on Dougie's bookshelf because he came across the chapter about a Shit Town fan. On those, thankfully, very rare occasions when they appear live on television, the game is unwatched, whoever the opposition, save for the odd glance at Teletext and, if the result is the right one, we'll happily watch the highlights of their defeat with unashamed delight. Obviously, we are not alone at our club in having these feelings. For a time, a friend of ours ran a business making the flags and banners so often seen at games and his little empire was soon flourishing. One day, the phone rang and a simple request from some sad git for a flag in blue, white and orange launched our friend into a torrent of abuse closely followed by the noise of the receiver being slammed down. The only other result we need to hear is theirs, and that they lost and are below us in the League (both, luckily, usual). Nothing else really matters: the constant chanting of 'We hate L*t*n' and 'L*t*n run from Watford' are testimony to our true feelings. Yet we sometimes wonder whether the staff at the club are aware of this feeling, and if they are, whether they react as we do. As we have already said, to the majority of players, a club provides a job, that is all, and it is only when a player approaches testimonial time that, we believe, this status is changed. That is fair enough, and we readily accept the situation, knowing that players will do their best for whoever pays their wages, but we neither accept nor understand how anyone can be transferred to a local rival and then just change allegiance at the stroke of a pen. How can they do that? Recently, rumours spread among the Watford fans that we were looking to sign a well-known ex-Shit Town striker and the club was besieged with irate fans. We would never allow it, not in a million years; we could never, ever have given our support to this player in any circumstances because we could not have trusted him. How could he do his best for us when he used to play for them? Loyalty runs very deep within football supporters; local rivalry, and therefore local loyalty, runs deepest of all.

There is an even uglier side to local rivalry, and that is of course, violence. If we have ever been to a local derby where violence has not taken place we cannot remember it, and at most such matches, home or away, it is expected and becomes an integral part of the day. The clubs and the police are well aware of this and before games will attempt to defuse the situation through the local press and supporters' clubs, but it will never work because to many fans these matches are just too important. On Merseyside, red and blue standing side by side may be the norm nowadays, but at my club, and at the majority of others who have local derbies like ours, it will happen when hell freezes over and only then after a decent period of reflection. Football is a game in which many things are dictated by tradition – England playing at Wembley and the FA Cup, for example – but hatred of other fans and in particular of local rivals is a tradition far stronger than any other. The feeling of giving the biggie to your most-hated enemy when your lads have just scored is what being a fan is all about, and for many, giving them a good hiding is an extension of that. Not a pretty thought, but a fact beyond dispute. Sadly, we at Watford are in a horrific situation because Shit Town are probably our biggest bogey team. We never seem to beat them, no matter how far above them we are in the League or whether we are at home or away, which gives our games an astonishingly cruel edge. When we have the grave misfortune to lose to them it destroys us and ruins an entire season, and that's another thing we hate them for.

Below are two accounts which typify Watford's dislike and distrust of 'the Scum', which are taken from the encyclopaedia of records stored in our memories. They are both humorous, because to have chosen anything more serious would have been to appear boastful, but we make no apologies for featuring them, just as we make no apologies for refusing to include anything sent by L*t*n fans to our box number. If that upsets any of them, so much the better.

Hijack

Back in the old days, about 1983, I think, I had an old Ford Zodiac which was my pride and joy. The best thing about it was that it could carry six people in great comfort and so it was adopted as our away-day transport and we went bloody everywhere in it. I think we went to something like twenty away games by car that year – the London ones were all by train – and we had a bloody great time. The best thing that happened that year was one of those incidents that come out when you're talking football in the pubs or at the games. It's something I will never forget because it was so bloody funny.

We were on our way to see the Golden Boys [Watford] play at Notts County and for once there were only five people in the old girl so there was even more room than usual. As we were getting on to the M1 at Hemel Hempstead, we looked to see if there were any of our lads hitching, but what did we see, only a Shit Town fan with his scarf on and his thumb out. We could not believe our luck. Here was a dream come true! We pulled over and he came running up. 'Are you going to L*t*n, lads?'

'Of course,' we cried. 'Dive in and we'll drop you at the Arndale' which is the shopping centre near the poxy little hovel they call a ground.

This poor bastard was so happy. 'I've only been standing there about five minutes. Thanks, lads. Do you go every week?' He was spouting out all this crap and we were nodding away. I mean, this prick must have been about seventeen or eighteen but he just didn't click on to what was happening. How we kept from laughing I'll never know. I suppose he started to become uneasy when I drove past the L*t*n turn-off in the fast lane at about seventy and he was mighty worried when the next two turnings went past as well because he was strangely silent.

'You are going to L*t*n, aren't you?' He asked the question, but he was already aware of the answer.

'We go to Shit Town once a year, mate, when Watford play there, and today, you're coming with us, my son. You're going to see the Hornets play, so just sit down, be quiet and don't you dare fuckin' move.' His face was a bloody picture. Not only was he not going to see his team but he was being taken miles away by people who supported the local opposition and there was nothing at all he could do about it. We just carried on talking as usual and this poor git had to spend an hour or so listening to how much we hated his team, his ground, their shit fans and their manager.

When we got to Nottingham, we stopped in the town and told him to get out and leave his scarf as a memento. 'You mean you're not going to take me back to Hemel?' The stupidity of that question has made me smile for over ten years. We drove off leaving this poor git on the outskirts of Nottingham. I have no idea how he got home – I don't really care – but he gave us the greatest laugh I have ever had at football. The look on his face when we drove off was absolutely classic.

A Fireman's Tale

If you want my favourite football story, here it is. I go to football with some great lads, all of whom have fairly good jobs – Christ, you have to have if you want to go to football these days, it costs so bloody much. Anyway, when we're at games or travelling, one of the things we talk about is how much we hate Shit Town and the things we would do to cause them or their fans the maximum grief if ever we got the chance. This has now started to move on into real life: one of our happy band is a solicitor and now refuses point-blank to represent any Shit Town fan because, in his words, 'I'd rather the cunt lost the case and went down.' Only recently, another of the lads almost landed himself in a row when he was out shopping with his wife. While he's standing at a sports clothing stall, this bloke comes up and asks for a Shit Town shirt for his nephew, who is a mad keen fan. My mate turns round and says, 'Well, you should get him a life, then, the sad little git,' to which this bloke, and his wife, took great exception.

The best story is one of the most recent and involves our top man, who happens to be a fireman. One night, they got a call to this house which was on fire, and they got there pretty bloody quickly in case anyone was inside, but as it happened, thankfully, they were all out. My mate was assigned to go in with the old aqualung on to put the fire out, so in he went through he front door with his hose on a wide-spray pattern to keep the heat off him. When he cleared the hallway, he started to move upstairs with his mate and on entering one of the still-burning bedrooms, what does he see? Only Shit Town posters on the walls and the happy face of Kerry fucking Dixon smiling warmly (pun intended) down at him. This tosser even had a Shit Town quilt cover!

Well, at this, he was of course outraged – I mean, this was against all his principles. So of course, he put the hose pattern on full power and blasted the shit out of this bedroom. To use his own words, 'Kerry Dixon and his mates went fucking everywhere, not to mention all the other Shit Town stuff this git had in his room, which was totally shagged when I had finished with it!' His boss went mad at him, but what could he do? The room was on fire and he had put it out. The young lad in question, who was about fourteen or so, was devastated, of course, and this was not helped when my mate told him to 'get real, grow up and watch a decent club'. Still, he does have a point as far as I'm concerned.

The following report is one of which explains all too clearly the frustrations felt by supporters of the smaller clubs. It was sent to us by a gentleman wishing to be known as 'the popular side dog'!

Bath City

Yesterday, my beloved Bath City played away at Staly-bridge Celtic in the last game of the season. Instead of doing the decent thing, the thing that most supporters would have done, I didn't go, and for one simple reason: because I've already been to Stalybridge. What I actually did was to sleep late and then go and get a paper. Now, I can't apologise enough for this – you've got every right to read this with disdain – but rather than go and watch my own team play, I decided to go ground-hopping. The *Western Daily Press* would tell me where I would be going.

I don't know why I went to Salisbury v. Wealdstone, an eighty-eight-mile round trip to a game I knew would provide dire football, but I had never been there and I just had to see the ground with people in it and teams on the pitch. As always, I dreamed about having a hot dog even though I'm a veggie, and, just like I normally do, I left at half-time because the game was indeed awful and spent the whole trip home searching for Bath's score on the radio.

The thing is, I just love football grounds; I love them more than sex, more than my job, more than anything. When my wife told me she was leaving me after five and a half years of marriage, I told her that I was going to see Cheltenham Town that day so could she please be gone when I got back and post her keys through the letterbox. On a recent business trip from Bath to Cornwall, I was given a big hire car and told to take my time getting down there and to bring my petrol receipts into the office when I returned. It was a Saturday, it was sunny and I felt like a kid locked in a sweetshop. I have always been fascinated by the Great Mills Western League, so in one day I saw the grounds which were home to Wellington, Elmore, Tiverton, Crediton, Okehampton, Tavistock, Plymouth Argyle (where I watched a 0–0 draw with Cardiff), Saltash, Liskeard, St Blazey and St Austell. I felt so exhilarated by the end of the day that I cannot begin to tell you, and the sense of achievement was overwhelming. I'm not an anorak – I just love football grounds, and ground-hopping is my escape from a job which is very high-pressure, takes me all over the world but pays me very well, and yes, I know, I am indeed lucky.

Even when I'm abroad I go hopping. In Sweden last year I spent a whole day looking for Hultsfred FC and I've had similar experiences in Holland, Greece, Belgium, Ireland and even in Japan. I usually know what I'll find in these places, but the pull on me is indescribable. There is nothing I've seen in the world quite so beautiful as the sight of floodlights on the horizon; the excitement is almost pornographic to me, I just have to peek through the fence, see the pitch and the terraces and gaze at the corner flags set up for the coming match. It doesn't matter to me if it's Old Trafford (and, yes, I have been to all the League grounds already) or Plain Ham (Larkhall FC, Somerset Senior League). It's a bit like churches, really, sometimes the small ones are better. I don't keep a little book or take pictures – I just have to know I've been there, you see. I look at the results in the sports pages of the *Mail on Sunday*, read the attendances before the results and imagine the 198 people at Marlow who watched them play Purfleet while secretly wishing that I had been number 199.

Now, this might seem like strange behaviour, and I suppose it is, but I tell you it all to explain a story. Sitting at home one afternoon, scanning the Teletext for football news as I do about ten times a day, I saw a news story that would change my view of football supporters forever. My favourite place in the whole world – Twerton Park, Bath – had been burned to the ground in an arson attack. Within seconds I was in my car and speeding to the ground as quickly as I could. There I found groups of old men standing staring at the blackened stumps sticking out of the ground and just crying. These were the men who had helped to build this ground (for just £662 in the 1930s) with materials nicked from the local factories at weekends and cranes which happened to find themselves mysteriously parked there by the workers of Stothart & Pitt, local people who were now just bewildered by the whole world because everything was gone – the offices, dressing rooms, bars, press box, everything. I felt devastated.

Briefly, what had happened was this. Six or so Bristol City fans, returning from some away trip, had got pissed, broken into the ground, poured petrol into the old wooden stand (which still had cleaners inside, and the lights were on) and put a match to it. The place went up immediately and all was lost. Those responsible were caught almost straight away as they ran into a drink-drive trap just down the road, and even the police managed to put two and two together for once. The reason for their arson attack was simple: Bristol Rovers play at our ground.

A few weeks later, I was in a print shop in Bristol and noticed that the guy behind the counter had some sort of T-shirt on under a thin white shirt. I made some joke about it and asked to see it. He opened his shirt to reveal a colour picture of a few guys being led along by some policemen. It was a real photograph alongside City's little robins logo with the words 'Bristol City Fire Brigade' underneath. I just felt sick. I rang Ashton Gate and complained, but they just attempted to disown this bloke. I asked them if they would let anyone into the ground if they found them wearing T-shirts like this and they gave me the usual load of old crap about these blokes not being proper supporters. Utter bollocks.

Now, I'm sure that there are proper City fans – we even get a few down to watch Bath City from time to time – but they do seem to have a surplus of complete wankers. Maybe it's that frustrated 'sleeping giant' thing (more like a comatose old piss-head if you ask me); maybe it's that Bristol seems to have more than its share of inner-city problems. Whatever it is, there is definitely something about that club. Even though we at Bath City don't like Rovers that much, we do at least get on and the ground-share has been pretty much a success. Maybe it's just that we are all so fond of daft old Twerton Park and put up with it, I don't know. But I do know that some of the people left standing in that car park after the fire have never been back, and that is a tragedy. To make anyone despair so much that he never goes to another game, to rob him of the love of his team, that's awful and terribly sad. I cannot understand how anyone can do anything like that, and if you ask me if I'm bitter, count on it, mate. If that's the mentality that exists within many League grounds these days, then I will continue to stay away. That's why I enjoy hopping so much. Violence isn't really a part of my football fever, it just seems remote and not a little stupid. I did see Canvey Island fans starting to get a bit lairy at Mangots-field, recently though . . .

We received a number of letters from supporters who some-times, for various reasons, watch other clubs and although we personally find this strange, when the occasion is a Wembley final even we would think about it. The letter below was sent to us from Steve of Croydon and illustrates perfectly the way that supporters, certainly those of us from the London area, follow their club, the South and then England, in that order. The famous North-South divide is alive and well.

A Day with the Dons

Although I now live in South London, my allegiances lie with a club in the Midlands. However, the day that Wimbledon got to Wembley, well, I just had to go, didn't I, and anyone who saw that game will know that there were huge numbers of Londoners who became Dons fans for the day, and I can see sod-all wrong with that. Actually, it was the only chance I have ever had to go to a game with all the lads I work and drink with as we all support different clubs, and so for us this was a big day out. It was quite funny because we had always talked about forming up a little mob and having a go, and here we were formed up and ready to rock and roll.

Anyway, before the game we went for the usual pre-Wembley drink and met up with loads of Dons who, although suspicious of us at first, accepted that we were there to support their club and welcomed us as such. I have to say that we had a great time with them. As we were all from different clubs, the stories came thick and fast, and we were soon into the top ten most hated grounds, clubs and players. It was not strange to hear that with one exception, Scousers came top of every list, the exception being my sad mate who travels to watch Everton. At about 12.30, something like fifteen Liverpool fans came into the pub, and although this immediately rang the warning bells for all of us 'newcomers', the Dons fans welcomed them as warmly as they had us and it soon became apparent that they were intent on having a great day out, and that they meant no trouble at all. So – and it went against the grain, I can tell you – we just joined in with everything that went on. Now, as anyone who's ever been to Wembley will know, on FA Cup day the TV build-up is compulsory viewing, no matter where you are, and the Dons lads really got off on watching their lads on the box. The atmosphere in the pub was fantastic until the Scousers came on and a couple of their lads started to get a bit mouthy about 'Cockney Wankers' and all that, something that always gets up my nose. But fair play, they were soon shut up by their own lads and everything got back to how it was.

At about 1.30, we started the move to the ground. As we left the pub, some of the Scousers started mouthing again. It was then that I realised that some of these bastards didn't have tickets and were after ours. They thought that the Dons fans would be an easy touch, but in this group of about forty Wimbledon supporters were our mob of about ten lads who were well up for it. No Scouse bastard would get near anyone's ticket if we had anything to do with it. As we walked to the tube, we realised that the Scousers were following. We held back from the Dons fans so that when they came, they would hit us first. That is exactly what happened. We heard them start running and were facing them before they got near us, and it was then that they realised that they had no chance, because we knew what we were doing. Being Scousers, by that I mean cowardly bastards, they stopped running at us, but before they could move again we went for them and they shit it big time. We only got hold of two of their lads, but they had the shit kicked out of them. They certainly knew they had been sorted and their mates just left them, the wankers. One of our lads was up for nicking their wallets and keys as well, which really fucks you up if it happens to you, but the Dons fans stopped us. They were really shocked by this; they hadn't expected, or wanted, any trouble at all. Wimbledon fans are hardly renowned for a mob, are they? But they were certainly glad we were there.

The walk up Wembley Way is one of the greatest feelings in football. Even though it wasn't my team, I felt proud to be there and, having fought for these lads, I felt as if I were one of them. We met up with loads of lads we knew from other clubs who, like us, had become Dons for the day, and it soon became apparent that the usual Scouse practice of mugging people for tickets had been going on since Friday night. Like us, they [the other temporary Dons] had been in rumbles with Liverpool fans, but unlike us, they had caught loads of them and taken tickets back. We even spoke to a couple of coppers outside Wembley, and they knew what had been going on but could do nothing about it because there was no way that they could identify the culprits – they had neither the time nor the descriptions. The poor bastards who had lost tickets were gutted, and a few of them were outside the ground in tears because they would miss their club's greatest day. The touts, of course, were loving this, and they must have made a fortune that day, although we saw a couple get turned over and have their tickets taken and handed out to Dons fans.

The game itself is history now. I can honestly say that I cheered that goal as much as any other goal I have ever seen in my life, and all of us were elated as we left the ground. It was one of those great footballing days. Walking back down Wembley Way, everyone was on a high, but the Scousers were devastated. Although loads of them were shaking hands with Dons fans, the younger ones were seriously pissed off and it was obvious that they would want a ruck before they went home. We were walking along with a group of about fifteen of them just behind us and the nearer we got to the tube, the more remarks we started to get from them. So we began to spread out, just enough to give ourselves room if they came at us. Suddenly, they started up the old 'Cockney wankers' stuff again and I stopped and turned to face them in the knowledge that the rest of my group would do the same. 'Come on, lads,' I said. 'No hard feelings, all right?' I walked forward with my hand held out, and although they stepped back at first, one of them came forward to shake my hand.

Now, if he was going to throw one at me, I'll never know as I got mine in first. Being left-handed, the second his hand was in mine, I pulled him across me and smacked him hard on the temple. Then, as he started to go down, I brought my knee into his stomach before I let go of his hand and he hit the deck. The rest of my group went for them with a vengeance and caught them before they could run. The lad I had done was out of the game so I went looking for another target, but all those who could had run and the rest were, shall we say, busy. Suddenly, from inside a burger bar across the road came loads of noise, and when I looked up, about ten more Scousers came out and were steaming across the road at us. Now we knew we would be in a ruck. The thousands of people in the road at that moment might as well not have been there because they sure as shit weren't helping us out. We knew there were no coppers because we had been watching for them when we started.

As they came at us I looked for blades, because Scousers are renowned for using knives and there was no way that I was getting cut. I couldn't see any so it was a case of shouting at our group to front them up. Now, although all this must have happened in seconds, like all rucks it seemed to take minutes, and we had time to get ourselves together and pick our targets before they hit us. But unlike the first lot, these boys knew what they were doing. Although I had picked a face for myself, as I moved at him someone else took me from the side and I went flying. I grabbed hold of him and took him down with me, holding him so that he couldn't get off and start kicking. Suddenly, the dayglo jackets were all over us. Fuck knows where they come from, but they took this lad off me and then threw us in a van before I knew what was happening. Within minutes, I was joined by fans from both sides and it became obvious that either loads of other people had joined in with this ruck or that the coppers had nicked anyone standing within thirty feet.

At the station, I pleaded innocence and pointed out at great length that Wimbledon fans were known for their good humour and lack of trouble, which was why I watched them, and that anyway, I had been attacked by this bloke as I went to shake his hand. The fact that the copper who nicked me confirmed that he had pulled off a bloke from on top of me helped my case, and after a couple of hours I walked out without a stain on my character and ready for a pint. Sadly, not all of our lads got away with it, but that's another story, and an occupational hazard. The fact remains that it was a great day out, probably the best I've ever had.

While working on this book we received a huge number of letters and met a great many people who told us a great many things, some scary, some interesting, some horrific, some fictitious and some wishful thinking. We also gathered together many accounts and observations that were highly amusing, because, after all, football spectating is basically a fun thing to do. But there was one letter which we felt just had to be in here somewhere. It has little relevance at all to this book, or to this chapter, except to show how football can become an overriding obsession to followers of local teams, and because it just made us laugh. We defy anyone to read it and not form a mental picture of the situation. It was sent to us anonymously, but we are certain that no one would write something like this if it were not true.

'Barnestoneworth'

One of the funniest footballing things I have ever seen was also probably one of the saddest. It was in 1977, and I was in the RAF working in Lincoln during the infamous firemen's strike. We had been covering the area for about two days and nothing had happened when we got a call to a house where the chimney was on fire. Now, for real firemen, chimney fires are bread-and-butter stuff but for us – well, we were shitting it. I mean, this was for real now. So we screamed to this house with two coppers on bikes escorting us, and when we got there, it was a typical *Coronation Street*-type two-up, two-down with the front door opening straight into the front room. The chimney was well alight. Not only that, but because it was our first fire, the local press were all over us and the pressure was really on to do everything just right. As the lads quickly got the gear out, I knocked on the front door and this little woman answered. 'Have you come to put out our fire then, love?' she said. 'Come in and I'll put the kettle on.'

Well, in I walked to find that this house was almost totally decorated with pictures of Lincoln City players. There were red and white scarves hanging on the back of the door, and above the fireplace was an aerial photograph of the ground. The man of the household, who had obviously just got in from work, was sat at the table eating fish and chips wrapped in newspaper reading the back pages of the local rag. It was just like a scene out of the famous Barnstoneworth United episodes of *Ripping Yarns*, and I couldn't help thinking that these people were indeed sad northern bastards of the type you only ever see in those bleak working-class dramas on television. 'Do you like football, then?' I asked in an attempt to make conversation, and off they went, telling me at great length that City were the greatest thing since sliced bread etc., etc.

While I was in the house talking to these two people, who were acting as if they didn't have a care in the world, my crew had got on to the roof and put a hose into the top of the chimney. The procedure with this sort of fire is to sprinkle water down and let the steam put the fire out, but remember, this was our first-ever call and we were very scared, so the lads sent the full lot through the hose. As I was stood in the front room, I suddenly became aware of the pump's engine note rising to a scream and then all hell broke loose as this chimney erupted and soot shot everywhere, closely followed by what seemed like about 200 gallons of water. This room, the couple, me and all the pictures on the walls were covered in black gunge, but the most hilarious thing was that this bloke just carried on eating his dinner as if nothing had happened.

I just cracked up, I couldn't help myself. Their room was totally ruined but the guy was still eating and the woman was so grateful that we had put the fire out I think she would have had my children if I had asked. I was so embarrassed and so were the lads, but she wouldn't hear of it when we offered to go back the next day and clear it all up for her. You just knew that she would have it all done by the time we got there, anyway. I would love to have the chance to go back, just to see if the house was still the same as when we arrived. Even to this day, when five o'clock arrives I always have a quick look at the Lincoln City result, think of that couple and remember that night.

Chapter 4
Racism

Almost everyone reading this book will, at one time or another, have had a conversation with someone who knows everything about football hooligans, but who has never actually been to a game. We have all met the type a thousand times – at work, in the pub, even at home – and they are a pain in the arse. They believe everything they read in the press about 'our' mentality and will not listen to anything we have to say because they believe us all to be illiterate morons, extreme right-wing, unemployed thugs from broken homes with criminal backgrounds. This, as we all know, is complete bollocks. It is no nearer the truth than to say that the average Scotsman wears a kilt, plays the bagpipes and is tight with his money or that the average Irishman is a thick, Guinness-drinking labourer.

The fact that this breed of fan exists at all is the fault of the media, the FA and the Football League, who for years have been responsible for perpetrating the ridiculous myth that football supporters are like sheep and should be treated accordingly. One only has to look at the lack of communication between clubs and their fans, and at the way that the FA has dealt with England's followers since the farce that accompanied the European Championships in 1988, to see that this is indeed the truth. However, there is one area in which these fine bodies have exceeded even their abysmal record in dealing with specific problems, launching campaign after campaign to try to sort it out. But, try as they might to convince the public that this problem is rife within British football at club level, the truth is that within the grounds and among those on the terraces or in the stands, it does not exist at anything like the level the football authorities and the politically correct movement would have us believe. That problem is racism.

To say that there are not racists among football fans would be horrifically naive, but in our experience racism is certainly less prevalent inside grounds than outside for the simple reason that we, as supporters, will worship anyone who gives their all for our team. Give me, or almost any fan from any club in the country, a centre forward who can bury the ball at will, or a defender with the ability to put Romario in his pocket, and I would let him come round to my house, eat all my food, drink the contents of my fridge and let him marry my eldest daughter no matter where he comes from or what colour he is.

There are clubs which have a history of having racist fans, but the constant highlighting of a problem that is obviously receding just stops people from visiting grounds and enjoying football. There is no doubt at all that a great many supporters from ethnic backgrounds have been, and remain, convinced that racism is rife within grounds due to these campaigns. Many of those coloured supporters who do go regularly, however, are decidedly unhappy about being looked upon as a 'special case' because that is just what they do not seem to want. We would even go as far as to say that football should be held up as an example of the positive things which can be achieved in society through sport, because to many people, especially children, players are heroes no matter what their colour. If you doubt it, look at the hordes of little white, black and Asian kids wearing their Cole, Yeboah or Shearer shirts with pride. There is certainly no racism in their minds.

So why is it that football is consistently attacked on this issue? There are two basic reasons. The first is that our game is not only a high-profile activity, but it is an easy target. No one in authority would dare to put the case that we are putting to you because most people are terrified of being branded a racist. We can well understand this fear, because racism does rank alongside paedophilia as a bad personal habit, but someone has to tell the truth. This misconception is something that is damaging football, and that is far from a good thing. The second factor which counts against us is the fact that supporters chant at games, and sometimes these chants are overtly racist in their content (media words, not mine). Bollocks.

It is important to understand why we shout and scream at football, because it is something that comes naturally to most of us. Football is by its very nature an emotive beast, and if things are not going right then the crowd will get on to the players, either of the opposition or their own team, in an attempt to provoke some sort of reaction. 'You dirty northern/southern/fat/black/bald/Cockney bastard' (take your pick), 'you Scouse twat' or 'you Scottish wanker' are all commonly heard examples which spring to mind, as are 'you useless git', 'you're shit' etc., etc. All of these comments are abusive, and none is very nice, but why is it that out of all those, one word in particular stands out as being more abusive than others? Is the word 'black' actually offensive to anyone? Nigger, Paki, honky and chinky are all abusive words, black is not. In all the insults listed above, the fan is picking on a distinguishing feature of a player. The abuse comes from calling him a 'dirty bastard', the 'fat/black' etc. description is used merely to show which player is the target.

However, some might argue that there is still a difference. For example, I am fat and bald, and people could choose to insult me by commenting on this. I could escape such insults by dieting and wearing a wig. This option is not available to a black person, and therefore the insult is worse. This is totally ridiculous, why would someone want to change their colour? Every coloured bloke I have ever met has been proud to be black and I'm sure if I went up to Les Ferdinand or Stan Collymore and asked them if they would rather be white, they would laugh in my face (at the very least!).

While we accept that, at times, throughout the seventies and eighties, coloured players must have had terrible times on the pitch, especially at certain grounds, things have changed. By their very presence, persistence and performances, players like Clyde Best forced people to accept them as great players rather than great black players. These days, of course, things are very different, because almost every team has black players in its squad. The colour of a player's skin is immaterial to the vast majority of supporters, which speaks volumes for the positive way racial equality has progressed within the game, and throughout society as a whole. What is needed is for football to take a different tack with this issue and look at the positive things that black and foreign players have brought to our game. For example, Ian Wright displays a positive attitude to any form of abuse and shows how it can be handled. He is at the top of the tree, a superb player who earns a great deal of money (which no supporter with any sense begrudges) and as such is an obvious role model for all young kids.

When Cantona lost the plot at Palace, I waited with baited breath to see how long it would be before someone played the racism card. It didn't take very long, because it was quickly realised that this defence would help get the public on Eric's side. It worked. Within days, the press and television were accusing the supporter involved in the incident of being a member of the National Front, though this was not proved. Nike took the same option in their television adverts, where Cantona asked us if we saw a footballer or a Frenchman. Well, after that incident, he looked to be either an idiot or a thug.

Surely football should campaign to promote the positive side of the game, rather than wring its hands about the negatives. Yes, there is widespread abuse of all players at football, but it signifies little except the emotion and frustration of watching a game. To most supporters these days, players are colourless and if you doubt that, ask yourself a simple question, not including the odd big-mouth who calls someone a black so-and-so, when was the last time you saw a truly racist incident at a game?

I can honestly say that, in all the years I have been going to football matches, other than Dublin which we will look at elsewhere, I have only ever witnessed one example of behaviour that I would describe as truly racist. For Watford supporters, a visit to West Ham in the golden days of Barnes and Blissett was not always a happy time. However, on one occasion I attended the fixture with my wife. As she is a Hammers fan, I took her to stand in the home end with the East End faithful. The arrival of the players on to the Upton Park pitch inspired the crowd to the usual taunts beloved of the Hammers, but the worst aspect of this response was the way in which grown men were talking to their young sons. Remarks such as 'Look, son, there's one of the black bastards,' and 'Look, boy, there's a jigger out there,' made me feel quite ill. The most disturbing thing of all was not the content of these verbal assaults – the white players and Watford supporters came in for their fair share of abuse – it was their ferocity. It was frightening to see people behaving in this way and it became even worse when Watford scored. It is something I have never forgotten, but that is the only time I have ever been aware of anything like it. I am certain that at the very small number of clubs which do still have a lingering racist element, a great deal of hard work is going on to remove what is after all only a tiny minority of supporters whose views are in no way representative of the vast majority of fans in this country.

While there can be no doubt that racism in any form is indefensible, be it at work or within sport, football supporters are merely football supporters. Therefore the game should not come under repeated attack as being the main home of this cancer. Inevitably, some individuals who go to football matches are racists, but it is a slur on all those who have worked so hard and achieved so much to say that the game is riddled by the problem. We supporters love the great game and we love those that play it, whatever nationality or colour they may be. What we supporters hate is people telling us what we are or what we should be, now that is what I call racist.

However, the subject of crowd abuse in general is yet another facet of football supporting which is once again under the spotlight. Having watched almost every game I've ever seen from behind a goal, hurling abuse comes as second nature to me and most football supporters for one reason: we love our clubs and we need them to win games – for us. When they play well, everything is perfect and they receive all the praise and adulation we can give them and they lap it up, but when they are bad . . . However, the opposition cannot expect any consideration. One of the reasons we're there anyway is to upset the other side in the usually vain hope that we will influence the result. Players know they will suffer abuse; it goes with the job.

If a player hears anything from the terraces that upsets him, well, frankly, tough. What about the heartache they've given us over the years? If they play crap, they leave the pitch feeling dejected and have a drink in the players' lounge, but we – the fans – leave the ground feeling destroyed, gutted, let down, frustrated and rejected. Watford have broken our hearts more than once, therefore we feel justified in giving them a bit of grief back from time to time. Isn't that just another part of the love affair? Players know that even though we're shouting all types of stuff at them on a Saturday afternoon, we'd still say hello if we saw them on Monday and then tell our mates who we'd seen in the street.

And why do people assume that the only targets for abuse are players? At Watford, Elton John was often on the receiving end of some choice words, as are most board members at some time or another. How often do Manchester United fans hear the *Dambusters* theme with all its connotations? We have also heard of Bradford fans being taunted by other supporters with burning pieces of paper which, while not very nice at all, is just another form of abuse designed to provoke a reaction. If you went into a sulk every time a visiting mob accused you of running from your local rivals, you'd never go again. But you know that, in reality, it isn't personal, it means nothing. The big question, however, is what gives us the right to hurl abuse. To us that is quite an easy one to answer. When I pay my hard-earned cash and walk through the turnstiles, I enter a place where all my troubles are forgotten. Here, there are no career, health or money worries; all there is is football and it gives us the opportunity to get rid of all our pent-up anger by shouting, cheering and singing. The man sitting next to me, or you, can be unemployed or a company director, it matters not a jot because for those ninety minutes we are all the same, with one common focus and we lose ourselves.

The game knows that and continues to sell itself to families on the basis of the 'big game' atmosphere while working hard to destroy it by clamping down on the chants and shouting. If you go into a pub, you expect to hear someone order a drink; go to a game and you expect to hear shouting, singing and swearing for it is that shouting, singing and swearing that creates the atmosphere, not hordes of nuclear families with 2.4 children clapping their hands as if they were at the circus. The game needs us, the hard-core of supporters, to be like we are and it needs to accept that fact before it is too late.

Of course, what we have been talking about here is club football. If you are discussing racism or abuse among supporters, the England team is an entirely separate area of debate. There can be no doubt that travelling abroad with the England team seems to instil a sense of national pride which too often manifests itself as hatred of everyone who is not English, whatever their colour. In this context, racism equates to nationalism, pride in the flag and hatred of all else. The extreme right-wing parties who target England games know that many supporters of the national side will adopt this stance at games. The Nazi salutes so sadly often seen among England fans are evidence that they do, although why they choose such an obviously foreign symbol to demonstrate their national pride still surprises us. The treatment handed out by the local police force never helps the situation. They will already have prejudged the English before their arrival and get their response in just as soon as they spot anyone with a Union Jack. This has the effect of stopping genuine supporters from travelling with the national team and therefore merely worsening the concentration of troublemakers. Ordinary fans are afraid of being stuck with this terrible label and no one can blame them for that.

Chapter 5
The Far Right

So football is a game which attracts all elements of society, for both good and bad reasons, yet there is no doubt that extreme right-wing (and more recently, left-wing) political parties use football as a recruiting ground for members. When England fans rioted in Dublin, the events were relayed around the world and, in the aftermath, a great many questions were asked regarding the events leading up to the game. However, it quickly became apparent that this was more than simple football violence, because a number of political groups were said to be heavily involved. We approached a number of these groups and asked them to contribute to this book. With one exception, they declined. Here is the account that was provided. After talking to many fans who were in Dublin that night, we do feel that this tale goes a long way to answering many of those questions, but, if accurate, the implications are very disturbing.

Dublin

I am an active member of the BNP [British National Party] and a follower of one of the smaller northern clubs, a club which has a growing reputation for good away support and an expanding hard core intent on causing as much trouble as possible on our travels. As an active member of

61

the BNP, I see the club as an ideal recruiting ground for new members and have been encouraged by the party to sell papers and distribute leaflets about our policies at all games, home and away. The party see football as a great place to canvass support as the majority of people who attend games are white British males who are finding life a bit of a struggle due to the lingering effects of the recession and the policies of the present political system which, we believe, are selling the very people who made this country what it was, i.e. great, down the river. It is our goal to reverse that decline by making people aware of what is going on so that we can make Britain great again. We manage to sell around 150 papers a month at the moment and the numbers are continuing to grow, which is obviously good for us and follows the trend of the last recession, when party numbers also grew.

There are, of course, many people at the club who are unhappy about us selling papers outside the ground and I know that a number of letters and phone calls have been received by the local press and the club and that some people are staying away because they do not approve of us. All I can say to that is that if they do not like our papers, then they shouldn't buy them – it is, after all, a free country. We have also had some grief in the past from groups like the Anti-Nazi League (ANL) and Anti-Fascist Action (AFA), but the lads in our group who do not agree with our beliefs will run with us against them as they see any attack on us as an attack on the reputation of the mob rather than on the party.

Being an organisation that suffers attacks from all sides due to its policies means that BNP groups from all over the country keep in close contact to exchange any information on factions campaigning in any way against us. The far-right parties do have a reputation for violence and when attacked they will respond in greater numbers, but Combat 18 [C18] (named after Adolf Hitler's initials – A=1, H= 8) is really an elite right-wing firm which holds a certain set of beliefs. They will travel anywhere and use violence and terror tactics on anyone who tries to stand up against what they see as their right. That does hold a certain fear factor for anyone who might think of trying to drive us out and away from the club. I know that there are many people who would like to do just that but would never dare attempt it, and would almost certainly never achieve it.

In February 1995, a group from our club travelled with some other BNP members from another northern club to the England match in Dublin. We had been encouraged for a few months previously to try as hard as we could to attend this game – not that we needed much encouragement: we have very strong feelings regarding Ireland and the current political situation, but we were concerned that we would be stopped at the airport by the police and prevented from travelling. We knew that they would be all over us and would know our arrangements, but we were assured on more than one occasion that they did not have the power to stop us. It was also mentioned that there were certain people involved who would see to it that we would make it to the match. At the time, I personally felt that this was all talk, but looking back on what happened, I do feel it could well have been true and that there were people who wanted us at that game.

Our objective was to try as best as we could to get to Dublin, to fire up the English support and, if at all possible, to disrupt the match in order to obtain as much media attention as possible. The whole point was to discredit the British government over the Anglo–Irish peace process. The media were televising the match live and there is nothing they like better than seeing the English supporters on the rampage, and we knew that as well as us, there were other groups who were doing their best to get to the game and put on a show.

England fans are different from your average club fans. They feel they have a point to prove, and what better place to prove it than Dublin, and against a team made up of players of every nationality you could think of whose manager can only be described as 'Judas' and a traitor to his country? England supporters are proud of the fact that they are English, and although the vast majority would not call themselves racist in any way, they are very nationalistic in that they love their country. Most of the ones I know feel that they should be treated with respect when they travel, and when this does not happen, they will go on the offensive and start to play up. The fact that most have been on the receiving end of bad treatment by the foreign police on more than one occasion does not help and it is very easy to spread bad feeling among England supporters if you really want to do it.

We were all surprised at how easy it was to get to Dublin. At the airport in England we had no problems and the same can be said of our arrival in Ireland. We actually travelled out on the Tuesday, along with a few other firms, and although there was a bit of grief along the way, this was just a continuation of some trouble at a Cup game earlier in the season. But I have to say that we were not attempting to hide the fact that we were England fans in any way whatsoever. Once we arrived in the city, we met up with other groups and the mood throughout was one of surprise that we were, in general, being left to get on with it. Rumour was out that a large number of C18 had arrived earlier in the week, having come via different routes to avoid being detected and deported, and that they were being looked after by members of the Ulster Freedom Fighters, one of the organisations with which C18 has established links since the introduction of the Anglo–Irish Agreement. That night we found a bar, settled in and kept being visited by small groups doing the rounds. They told us that a few of the English fans were fighting among themselves but that it was all very quiet, really, as the locals had no intention of getting involved in anything.

On the day of the match, we found ourselves joined by many familiar faces and the number of England supporters grew steadily, which meant that the atmosphere grew more hostile by the minute. News of pubs being decorated with Loyalist slogans, plus the odd fight, helped to generate the kind of feeling we were expecting to find at such an important fixture. There was plenty of BNP literature being distributed and most of the talk was not about the football, but about what was going to happen once we were inside the ground. Anybody could have seen the intention that day and everyone involved was getting well fired up.

When we left the pub, we marched to the ground and for the first time started to put on a bit of a show. We had accumulated a large mob by now and it looked as if the police just wanted to get us off the streets and into the ground as quickly as possible. The security system they had set up was a joke. It just did not work – we went straight through them and up to the turnstiles. It was at this point that I started to believe that we would actually make it as up to then I had been half expecting a tug at any second.

Inside the stadium the atmosphere was electric, full of violence, expectation and hate. As well as the usual faces there were a lot of boys I had never seen before whipping it up. What also surprised me was that there were Irish supporters in the same section as us and, as a consequence, they were getting punched and kicked at random. The police seemed powerless to stop it, so many of these Irish fans started to leave. As kick-off time grew closer, the chants of 'No surrender to the IRA,' and 'Ulster is British' predictably became louder and you could clearly see how the majority of the English fans were being manipulated by the number of BNP members present. (This may seem an odd thing to say, but I personally believe that the majority of English people feel the same way as we do on most things but need to be with like-minded individuals or groups before they are prepared to stand up and say what it is they really think.)

Some of the English lads were wearing balaclavas, which

is a bit unusual for us, but these, together with a few others, had by now begun throwing things down on to the people in the section below. We had well and truly arrived, and it quickly became obvious that we were in total control of that part of the stadium and had really stirred everyone up. It was clear that it was going to go off big-time, and with the attention of the media fully upon us by now, we suddenly realised that here was the chance for us to let the world know how we really felt about Northern Ireland. Football had given us the moment, but the game itself had become what it always is for us: secondary to the objective which we had set out to achieve. As I have said, our initial aim was to disrupt the match, but by now we were getting confident that we could actually get the game abandoned.

As the Irish anthem played, we did our best to drown it out with 'Sieg Heils' and other singing while the police were still leaving us to get on with whatever we wanted. It would have taken a very brave, or very stupid, policeman to step into such a mob and try to drag someone out at that point, and this lot did not seem ready to do it at all. By this time, people were starting to rip up the seats and arm themselves because most of us were expecting the riot police to come in at any moment, which would have been the signal for it to really kick off. As it was, things took a different direction when the Irish scored. It sent some of the lads off and suddenly there was total mayhem.

I remember thinking that these pictures would be going out live in pubs and clubs all over Britain and that most places in Europe would also be watching. That gave me the biggest buzz I have ever had at a football match. Most of us could see the fans below running on to the pitch and there were fights breaking out as they were both English and Irish, but that didn't matter to us at all because we had a political point to make. I must say, though, that once the riot police started to target the English lads on the pitch, we started to feel different and began to turn our attention towards them. It was a while before we realised that the players had been taken off, and then the announcement came that the game had been abandoned. The feeling of power that gave us was incredible. We had achieved more than we could possibly have hoped for, because news of this would travel around the world. The feelings of the BNP were well and truly known and the fact that we could orchestrate such an event would send a strong message to our opponents. The BNP would no longer be ignored and would be talked about at every breakfast table and at every place of work the following day.

Once the ground was clear and we had burned ourselves out, we were introduced to the riot police. It was clear that they wanted us out of the stadium and, I suspect, away from the media eye as quickly as possible. As we left, they directed us to the ferry port and we were escorted by policemen who were more than a little unhappy by this time. The fact that we were starting to buzz again did not help, and we were now giving out as much verbal as we could to anyone we saw. As we had travelled by plane, we tried to break away from the escort but the police told us that arrangements had been made for us to be taken to the airport from the ferry terminal. But when we arrived at the port, they kept us hanging about for a while and then told us to get on the boat. When some of the lads started to play up about wanting to go to the airport, the police began to get heavy and hit out with their batons. We could see that things were starting to get a big dodgy because the police were singling people out for hidings and so we decided to run on to the ferry and travel that way. Looking back on it, I hate to think what would have happened had we insisted on being taken to the airport. As it tuned out, the boat was quite a laugh because the buzz was still going and many of the BNP groups were on board, and although a few people had taken a beating, the mood was unbelievable. When we arrived back in Holyhead the media circus was in full swing, but we avoided the attention. There's always someone who is prepared to have their face flashed across the TV screens, but it isn't me.

The thing that really surprised us about this whole incident was the cover-up in the British press over the next few days. At first most of the daily papers carried stories about the BNP involvement in starting the whole thing off as well as giving coverage to C18, but within days that had been taken out of the equation and it was merely 'football fans' with the same tired old clichés. No mention of the Far Right, our objective or the political situation which was the catalyst for the whole thing. I still find it unbelievable that the game was staged in the first place, and I'm sure that the government were aware of what was almost certainly going to happen from the minute the fixture was arranged. The police in both countries must have voiced their concerns all along, but still it went on and we were allowed to attend. Maybe we were just meant to be there.

PART THREE
Behind the Matchday Madness

Chapter 6
The Firms

During your spectating life, you will invariably find that you end up going to games with, or sitting with, the same people for almost every match. In the vast majority of cases, it is a bloody good laugh, nothing more, nothing less. You may never see them except at football but once you are inside that little group, at home or away, or even in the pub for the pre-match or post-match pint, they are as important to you as your own family. For many fans, that is one of the main attractions of the game anyway – meeting new people with the same interest but with whom they have no connection in their everyday lives. It's just another part of their escape into the world that is football.

Now, this is all well and good for most people, but what if you and your little group like to indulge in the odd bit of trouble? What if, for example, you start going to games with your mates at an early age and basically grow up together; you start travelling and you start fighting, and, sooner or later, you get sick of being on the defensive all the time, so you start attacking and planning. You get organised, and before you know it, you're all in your twenties with a reputation.

Let's look at another scenario. You're in a pub with a load of other blokes – you go there before every home game and have done so for a couple of seasons – and it gets hit by a group from the opposing team and some of you take a serious hiding.

71

When your club plays the same team away the next season, you and your mates go up there and do the business on their pub to get your revenge. But then they come back to your place, and so it goes on.

And another: you live in a small town without a real team of its own, so you go to watch a League side a few miles away and there are plenty of others who do the same. You travel on public transport with the same people every week, get to know all of them and end up standing together in the same place at every game. That becomes your place. Over the seasons, as you get older, you start to organise your own coaches to take you to matches and end up travelling away a lot.

All these situations have arisen at almost every club in England at some time or another and have formed the basis of nearly every organised group in this country. Inevitably, these gatherings will contain the odd bunch that is more active than most when it comes to violence. It may not be organised initially, but they will not recoil from a scrap and will put themselves about to such an extent that they will begin to get themselves known to the rest of the home fans, and the seeds of a reputation will be sown. The people in this group will soon realise this and they will be extremely proud of the fact that, rather than being just anonymous individual spectators, they are now a recognised faction within the club. So they work hard to grow, because, above all else, they want that reputation to develop. As a result the fights they have will become fiercer and the raids more daring. There may only be ten of them, there may be fifty, but they feed off that reputation and the fear they hold for other people while the buzz they get when forming up on matchday – as well as before, after and during any trouble – becomes addictive.

So now you have your fame among the home fans and you have decent numbers. You know that probably less than half of you will be what you would call the hard core, while the rest will be at best reliable and at worst cling-ons or glory-hunters. But you want the firm to grow; you need new members, so how does that happen? Well, at some clubs it just won't, because the hard core do not want it to. They know that it is easier to organise twenty people than 200, and they also want to maintain their elitist aura. They know, too, that small groups can do more damage than big ones most of the time. But the most important factor is that the more people you have in a group, the more chance there is that its reputation will be damaged or even lost by people doing a runner when faced with a dodgy situation. For most groups, though, it is inevitable that eventually the membership will increase because people will attach themselves; people like to belong.

However, no one is going to walk into any firm and be immediately accepted. It just does not happen, as the undercover police have found to their cost on many occasions. Anyone joining a group does so from the outer edges. He must gain a reputation of his own and some respect from those on the inside before he is likely to be taken seriously, and it can take many seasons and many battles before that happens. The reputation of the group, the most important thing of all, is in the hands of every member and each of them must have the utmost faith in the others to maintain it, just as the hard core have complete trust that every other member will back them up during any 'offs'. There are other ways to join a firm. Newport County supporters, for example, once ran a recruitment drive among the fans by putting up posters around the town. (We also believe that Newport had a group made up entirely of females, which obviously means that membership is somewhat restricted.) There are also cases where people have been invited to join other groups (even at a different club) because of their own individual reputations and what we will call 'connections'. We are also aware of separate groups from the same club who will join up to travel and fight, or travel separately but fight together, although they will never merge completely because one of them would have to give up its own history and reputation. However, these opportunities are rare, and for the majority, the only way into a group is on merit, and earning that takes time, hard work and dedication.

Once your firm gets into a position where it has some status among other clubs (good or bad, depending on your viewpoint), you will unavoidably get other groups trying to damage what you have built up. As we have attempted to show elsewhere, it can get to the stage where your own result is at least as important as that of the team you follow. You know that if Cardiff or Birmingham come to town, you will be well tested, just as they expect to be tested. That's the game; that's what it's all about. Of course, it isn't only at matches that things happen: every club has people who will indulge in violence, whether it's a large club like Middlesbrough, which has some of the most violent supporters in the country, or a smaller one like Wigan Athletic, whose fans will be ready to turn you over big-time. The Football League tables have absolutely no relevance to the organised groups. As any supporter will happily tell you, running the gauntlet of the London underground or the northern rail network can be a very dangerous business indeed, because you never know who you will meet – and organised firms from smaller clubs can be very dangerous indeed.

Now, it is one thing to have a reputation with your own supporters, but the groups want to be known to other clubs, they want *their* exploits to be talked about. There is one thing above all else which will help that cause: a name. It doesn't matter where it comes from or even how stupid it is, because once it is known it will spread like wildfire if the group is active every week. If you are unlucky enough to get involved in an incident where you're on the receiving end, getting a calling card thrust into your hand which says something like, 'Congratulations, you've just met the Chelsea Headhunters,' ensures that the name of that group will be known throughout your club in a matter of hours. The calling card is a great tool which is used by most mobs these days, and the availability of printing machines at post offices and railway stations makes them easy to obtain and totally untraceable.

What follows is a list of names of firms gathered and given to us by two people who have assisted us with our research. It is clear that many clubs have more than one named group, but the list is by no means complete because new outfits are being formed and developing all the time.

It will nevertheless give some idea of the range of clubs which have firms attached to them and which may well be meeting your team some time in the near future. For the record, Wigan Athletic, who have an average attendance for home games of about 2,000, recently took a firm of approximately 400 to Blackpool for a pre-arranged 'meeting'. And you thought we were joking?

Arsenal	Gooners
Aston Villa	Steamers, Villa Youth
Barnsley	Inter-City Tykes, Five-O
Birmingham City	Zulu Warriors
Blackburn Rovers	Blackburn Youth
Blackpool	BRS (Bison Riot Squad), Seaside Mafia, BTS (Blackpool Tangerine Service)
Bolton Wanderers	Tonge Moor Slashers, Mongoose Cuckoo Boys, Billy Whizz Fan Club
Bradford City	The Ointment
Brighton & Hove Albion	Headhunters
Bristol City	Inter-City Robins
Burnley	SS (Suicide Squad)
Cambridge United	Cambridge Casuals
Cardiff City	Soul Firm
Carlisle United	BCF (Border City Firm)
Chelsea	Headhunters
Chesterfield	CBS (Chesterfield Bastard Squad)
Darlington	Darlington Casuals, Bank Top 200, The Gaffa, Under-5s, The Townies
Derby County	DLF (Derby Lunatic Fringe)
Doncaster Rovers	DDR (Doncaster Defence Regiment)
Exeter City	Sly Crew

Fulham	Thames Valley Travellers
Grimsby Town	CBP (Cleethorpes Beach Patrol)
Hereford United	ICF (Inter-City Firm)
Huddersfield Town	HYC (Huddersfield Young Casuals)
Hull City	City Psychos
Leeds United	Service Crew
Leicester City	Baby Squad, MMA (Matthew & Marks Alliance), BIF (Braunstone Inter-City Firm), TRA (Thurnby Republican Army), ICHF (Inter-City Harry Firm)
Lincoln City	LTE (Lincoln Transit Elite)
Manchester City	Maine Line Service Crew, Guv'nors
Manchester United	Inter-City Jibbers, The Cockney Reds
Middlesbrough	Frontline
Millwall	Bushwackers, The Treatment
Newcastle United	Bender Crew, NME (Newcastle Mainline Express)
Northampton Town	NAT (Northampton Affray Army)
Nottingham Forest	Red Dogs, Naughty Forty
Oldham Athletic	Fine Young Casuals
Oxford United	Warlords
Peterborough United	PTC (Peterborough Terrace Crew)
Plymouth Argyle	Central Element
Portsmouth	657 Crew
Reading	Berkshire Boot Boys
Rotherham United	Rotherham Casuals

Sheffield United	BBC (Blades Business Crew)
Sheffield Wednesday	OCS (Owls Crime Squad)
Shrewsbury Town	EBF (English Border Front)
Southampton	Inside Crew, The Uglies, Suburban Casuals
Stockport County	The Company, Hit Squad
Sunderland	Vauxies, Seaburn Casuals, Boss Lads, The Redskins
Swansea City	Swansea Jacks, Jacks Army
Tottenham Hotspur	Yiddos, N17s
Tranmere Rovers	TSB (Tranmere Stanley Boys)
West Bromwich Albion	Section Five
West Ham United	ICF (Inter-City Firm)
Wolverhampton Wanderers	Subway Army, Bridge Boys
Wrexham	Frontline
York City	YNS (York Nomad Society)

This book is mainly concerned with clubs within the English League structure, but Scotland, too, despite what the media would have you believe, has its fair share of football violence. Every England fan will be only too aware of what the Scottish are capable of. Those famous pictures of them swarming all over London and the Wembley pitch make me feel ashamed, and pre-season visits by both Rangers and Celtic have left their mark on many grounds in this country. The links that have been developed between English and Scottish firms (Manchester United/Celtic and Chelsea/Rangers are the two most obvious) seem to be more political or religious than football-related, but they will join up, and indeed have, to fight together when the need arises. Below is a list of Scottish firms that we know are active at this time.

Aberdeen	ASC (Aberdeen Soccer Casuals)
Arbroath	Soccer Crew
Celtic	Celtic Casuals

Dunfermline Athletic	CSS (Carnegie Soccer Service)
Heart of Midlothian	CSF (Casual Soccer Firm)
Hibernian	CCS (Capital City Service)
Montrose	No Casuals, Portland Bill Seaside Squad
Motherwell	SS (Saturday Service)
Glasgow Rangers	ICF (Inter-City Firm)
St Johnstone	FCF (Fair City Firm)
St Mirren	Love Street Division

Within many firms, every fixture has its own history. A particular game, which might date back many years, will be uppermost in every supporter's mind on matchdays. The letter reproduced below was sent by Stuart from Barnsley, and shows just how one such rivalry began.

The ICT

On this particular day (10 September 1983), Barnsley's Inter-City Tykes (now known as the Five-O) had turned out in good numbers as word had spread that 'Boro's Frontline crew were highly respected and, it was said, harder than Newcastle. This, in the eyes of most Barnsley folk, was quite an achievement, as the Geordies had virtually wrecked the town during the 1981–82 season. Previously, matches against 'Boro had seen only minor trouble, but this season saw a fierce rivalry develop which is just the same today.

The Barnsley mob had arranged to meet in the town centre at about 11.30 but our plans were foiled when elements of the Frontline began arriving at about 10.30. At eleven, myself and a few friends declined the invitation [to fight] of a group of about eight 'Boro supporters, two of whom brandished Stanley knives, when they shouted over to us as we walked past the local Woolworth's. By midday, a group of about forty to fifty of the Barnsley mob had gathered in the Corner Pin pub and like us, many had stories about 'meetings' with 'Boro lads in the town. It was time for action. One of our lads was sent out to find out where the 'Boro had congregated while another rounded up the remainder of the ICT, most of whom were sat in the upper sections of The Chennells, which is another pub in the town. At about 12.20, the word was out that 'Boro were on Kennedy Street and so off we went with the adrenaline pumping and that warm feeling, the glow of anticipation, growing in my stomach. This was going to go off, and it was going to be big.

At first the Barnsley mob, which by now was about 100 to 120 strong, moved slowly, but by the time we were halfway towards our target, we were at a brisk walk. As soon as we set eyes on our rivals, who were about fifty strong, we set off at a charge and when they saw us, they fanned out across the road to make their stand. 'This is it,' was all I could think, and within seconds, both mobs were trading punches and kicks. I took a few good slaps and my head felt like it was on fire, while my right eye was numb. I was then knocked over a fence with a cracking blow which I didn't even see coming. The 'Boro mob had stood their ground and given us a hiding, but while we felt that we had let the town down, we had to agree that they were a serious firm.

For the remainder of the day they held the upper hand in the town and also in the streets near the ground. About 100 of them wrecked The Mount public house and then went on to The Dove, which also got turned over. Inside the ground, they obviously felt that they could get another result but we had a good go back at them and actually chased about thirty of them on to the pitch when they tried to take a section of our end. This led to the kick-off being delayed for about five minutes. However, I have to admit that 'Boro really did take Barnsley that day, and big-style.

For the return fixture at Ayresome Park later in the season we had distributed leaflets in the town centre pubs, and on the day of the match we had a mob of about 250 lads heading to Middlesbrough for revenge. However, things did not go according to plan and, at about two o'clock, the Frontline attacked The Wellington pub, which is where we had all gathered, and five Barnsley fans were slashed with scalpels in the pub doorway before the 'Boro fans vanished. Because of this incident, Barnsley have held a grudge against Middlesbrough, but in all honesty, we have never really had the upper hand, although during the away game in the '89–90 season we did put up quite a show at Ayresome Park.

Some rivalries last many seasons and can stem from various origins. In other cases, violence can continue from encounters earlier in the season. The account below was sent by West Ham supporter Dave E., and explains one such experience.

Zulu Army

If you're looking for my favourite row story, well, there is only one candidate, and that has to be the two games we played against Birmingham back in 1982. We had, as usual, planned everything out and the lads had done an excellent job of finding out where their mobs went before the game and all that stuff. At that time, much as they do now, Birmingham had a serious reputation, but although we were concerned, we were confident of a result. We had to make our mark but we did know two things: it would be heavy, really heavy; and we would go tooled up.

For once we went by train – first class, of course, no second-class bollocks for us. This was because Birmingham is just a shit-hole and it's easy for the law to stop you on the motorways before or after the game. Anyway, we got to New Street and poured off the trains – there were hundreds of us – and suddenly it all kicked off, I mean, we've been there about two minutes! From what we saw, they had planned an ambush and it had gone exactly to plan. The trouble was, they hit too early and got trapped by the rest of our mob. We hit them with the full armoury – nuts and bolts, coins, everything we had brought with us – before we went steaming in with the old feet and fists and kicked the shit out of them.

It wasn't long before the Bill came in and nicked a few of our lads, but they turned up at the ground anyway, so we couldn't work out what that was all about. But that was it, because our carefully laid plans went out the window. The Bill were all over us like a rash and marched us to the ground like some bloody army regiment or something. Once we were inside, it all went off again, but they took a bit of a hiding, really, because they didn't have any real boys in there. We were quite disappointed that they were so crap; I mean, they had a reputation.

After the game we got back to New Street and it all went off again, big-time. They came from bloody everywhere and it was tremendous – I've never been in anything like that before or since. They had really got it together and hit us from every direction, first with the missiles – nuts, bolts, nails, that kind of stuff – and followed that up with wave after wave of bodies. No wonder they call themselves bloody Zulus! The coppers were shit – it was just us and them until the Filth got their act together – and we gave them a right spanking. It was only the next day that I found out that someone was stabbed, which is right out of order. If you use a blade you deserve to go down for it. This stabbing told us that they would try to take revenge big-time when they came to Upton Park, and we just could not let that happen. No one takes liberties at our place, no one.

To be fair, they had a big mob when they came down, but we had our plans ready and everything went well. Some of their coaches were done on the way to the ground but the bulk of their mob came by train and we had plenty of bodies waiting for them at Euston. Basically they fought their way to East London. It was heavy in the ground as well – we had loads in with them and there was lots going on. I remember that the game was held up for a time, so it must have been quite bad. After the match the Bill kept them in, which gave us time to get to Euston to give them a nice send-off. They still got plenty on the way because there was a load of Hammers with them, but it was when they came into Euston and saw us that it really went wild, especially as there were other clubs waiting for trains as well. I think that their mob even joined up with some other northern clubs to try to run us out, but by then, all the London clubs were in it together and it was bloody manic. That was a great day, but sadly, the law are on top of that sort of thing now, and it's just too dodgy now unless you want to go down. Fuck that for a caper!

Most supporters at home games will be aware of the reputation of visiting fans and will behave accordingly. The problems really start when you get trouble from a totally unexpected source.

Reading

I run the pub about 10 yards from the home turnstiles of our local club, which means that on matchdays, mine is the place where the bulk of the home mob gather before games. I don't really like football myself, but that's neither here nor there, because there is no way I'm going to tell you who or where I am. I like my pub and my licence too much! Anyway, now that's clear, I'd like to tell you about something that happened recently.

It was a normal Saturday game, with Reading the visitors, and, with the greatest respect to them, they were not what I considered to be much of a threat, crowd-wise, even though their team were doing well in the League at the time. Before the game I had the pub full of the usual lads with a couple of blokes on the door to make sure that no one got in who shouldn't. Everything was as usual, with the usual singing and pre-match noise, stuff like that. About 2.50 they all shot over to the match and gave me a couple of hours' peace before the regular, and I have to say profitable, Saturday-night post-game inquest.

During the game I had the usual visits from the local police, who call in and give me the lowdown on any trouble they've had or expect, as well as to have a couple of halves if they can. On this occasion, they told me that things had been getting a bit naughty in the town centre. The Reading fans had been moving around in little mobs and had been playing up a bit. So far they hadn't nicked anyone, but they warned me that things might get a bit heavy after the game, although they would be keeping them in for longer than usual to make sure that our lot were either in the pub or had been dispersed. At about four o'clock, this inspector came in and told me that the Reading fans had been talking to each other on walkie-talkies and actually coordinating their plans and movements. What this meant was that all these little mobs were really one big mob, and they were planning something major for after the game, although the police didn't know what yet. He then said that they would have more coppers on duty outside the ground just in case, and that he would let me know if anything else happened.

At this, I started to get worried. My little pub ain't much, but at least it's mine, and although the coppers would try to prevent it, there was always the chance that some wanker would lob a bottle or something through the window, which was not really what I needed. The other thing that got to me was that if a little club like Reading were at it like this, what were some of the bigger clubs up to? Being opposite the ground as I am, my place is a bit of a prime target, and although I've been here a bloody long time, you never get used to things like that. All I could do was wait and hope that the coppers would get their act together.

After the game, which ended in a draw, I think, all the home lads started to pour in and the place was filled pretty quickly. After about ten minutes these three coppers came in and told me to get the shutters down and lock everyone in as the Reading fans are about to total my pub. The coppers had heard them on their radios planning to go into town, double back out towards the ground and steam into my place. Well, all the lads went mad, and although the copper tried, he couldn't calm them down. There was no way that they were going to let anyone wreck 'their' pub, especially with them locked inside. So they all steamed out and poured into town, looking for the Reading mob, who probably had no idea that their plan had been rumbled and they would soon be facing about seventy outraged local fans intent on trouble.

Obviously, the police had to get on top of the situation. Apparently they blocked off the roads so that our lads were held in one place until they calmed down. But by this time the Reading fans had managed to lose the police, and, from what I heard, mobbed up inside one of the big stores in the town. The manager must have wondered what was happening when about 100 football fans suddenly appeared in his bloody shop. If he had known about it he might have been able to do something about it.

Anyway, it appears that the leaders of this mob then decided to get away from the town centre and so they all moved off, but as they found nobody about, they went into the pub right next to the railway station. My mate, who runs this pub, said that they just steamed in, attacked almost everyone who was inside, totalled the place within about ten seconds and were gone before he could do anything. As you can imagine, he went mental at the police when they finally arrived because they hadn't been following this mob, despite knowing full well that they were up to something. All the police wanted to do was to get them on the trains and out of the town as quickly as possible. Mind you, he hasn't found out yet that they were really after my place instead of his. That really will piss him off!

Of course, not every plan is a success, and the story below, sent to us by a Leicester City supporter, is a case in point.

Ambush

Our club, like most others, I suppose, has one team we hate above all others. It's not our local rivals, but Chelsea, a team which everyone who watches our club hates with a vengeance because they have turned us over, home and away, and always cause trouble in the town when they play here. I have no idea when it all started, but it was certainly a big game around the time I began coming to matches, which was a good few years ago now, but everyone agrees that this lot are southern bastards of the first order.

A few seasons ago, our team actually had a decent-sized mob at most games, and in the build-up to our match with these scum it was obvious that for once we had a chance of getting one over on them. But it would have to be planned with military precision. A few of us who drank in a pub near the ground started talking about ways in which we could hit them, and word got round that we were getting a mob together. We soon ended up with about fifty lads ready to do the deed. If nothing else, this shows you how disorganised we were, because if fifty blokes could get wind of our plans, the police could have heard about them just as easily. But we never had a whisper from them, so I suppose they never heard anything. Anyway, we talked about all sorts of ways we could get them, but it was obvious that we couldn't take on their mob face to face because they were experienced boys. We would have to ambush them in one way or another, and that was the plan we came up with.

On the day of the game we all met up early and set everything in place. Our plan was to start harassing them from the minute they got off the motorway and before they got under the protection of the police, who always met visiting coaches at exactly the same place. As the first coaches pulled off the slip road, one of our lads timed it so that he was driving past the junction, forcing the first coach to stop and let him past. The second it stopped, one of our lads ran out and threw a tin of paint across the windscreen while someone else opened the door and threw in a smoke canister, which instantly fucked up the entire coach and blocked the road. These lads then vanished as quickly as possible and got back into the town to meet up with the rest of us.

The first part of our plan had been accomplished, we had stopped the coaches for a while, and now we wanted the rest. We knew that most visiting fans drank in the same pub on the outskirts of the town and that was our next target. When we arrived, we found two or three of our lads who had been watching the place and could tell us how many of their lot were in the pub, but more importantly point out the cars they were in, because they were what we wanted. It goes without saying that the plan was to slash the tyres of every visiting fan, again causing maximum aggravation to them. It may seem childish, but that was all we could do. As we started to move into the car park, someone spotted us and they came pouring out, about thirty of them, which was about the same number of lads as we had. Although our plan was up the creek, we were faced with the chance of a ruck. Usually we would have gone for it, but this club in particular is known to have some vicious boys, and some of our lot bottled it and did a runner, leaving about twenty of us to front them up. We got a bit of a slapping for our pains and got out of there as quickly as possible.

After this near-miss and our previous exploits at the motorway, we soon attracted the attention of the Law. So, with kick-off time approaching, we headed for the ground to find that the game had been held back because of what they called 'traffic congestion' but which we knew was a result of our handiwork. During the match there were a few offs with some of their lads who had come into our end, but for once our lot seemed to come out on top. But after the game was something else. It was obvious that the disruption we had caused before the match had pissed off a lot of people and this had not been helped by some of the songs we had been singing during the game. It seemed as though every one of their supporters wanted us sorting out and they were up for it. The atmosphere was electric as we walked up the road away from the ground.

Rather than take the chance and vanish before either the police or, worse, their mob got hold of us, we did the stupid thing and started to gather at a point about a quarter of a mile from the ground near the main road out of the town. We took great delight in waving at the traffic and hurling abuse as the scum went past. We knew that they couldn't do anything because there was no way they could stop. Suddenly, this noise erupted behind us and we spun round to find about thirty of their lot coming at us, trapping us between them and the main road on which traffic was speeding past. We were fucked. The only thing we could do was run, either at them or through the traffic and of the two, they seemed the lesser of the evils. So we turned and steamed towards them in the hope that they would break ranks, but they didn't. The only thing this did was to get us to them faster, giving them more time to kick the shit out of us, which is exactly what they did.

Not one of our lot left that scene without being damaged in one way or another. As for me, it was about a week before the swelling went down and I was able to walk without limping. The only thing we accomplished that day was to upset the police, the local press and the club with our antics as well as ensuring that this particular club will go to town every time they play us, the bastards. But at least we had a pop, which is something, I suppose.

Chapter 7
The Scouts

It is obvious to most people who observe football supporters that many of the incidents involving violence are akin to military manoeuvres, and as many a military historian will tell you, any army is only as good as its intelligence. The police apparently spend a great deal of their time gathering information on football violence and trying to deal with it accordingly, and various academic research groups gather information and dispense reports which, usually, make laughable reading. The gathering of information for the established and organised football firms, meanwhile, is the job of the scout, who plays one of the most respected, and most dangerous, parts in the organisation of football violence. The men who carry out this role are usually fairly nondescript, but to them it is an advantage to look like an average bloke watching a match. They nearly always work in pairs, and although they are almost invariably men, we did meet one bloke who regularly scouted with his girlfriend. He assured us that people left him alone if he was with a woman. Their job is exceedingly sinister, for they are the people who provide the plans and locations that enable the team leaders to formulate attacks and ambushes when travelling away, and woe betide them if their information is wrong, because the crew could end up taking a hammering which will damage and might even destroy a hard-won reputation. The story of the

Chelsea firm which left Leeds after a game and then went back in at night to hit a nightclub, only to go to the wrong place and receive a serious hiding, is a case in point.

A good scout is worth his weight in gold, and he will be totally dedicated to the cause of his club – he has to be, for it is very rare indeed for him to watch his own team play away. He is always one or two matches ahead, watching and noting what the opposition mobs are up to, where they drink and how they get to grounds. If he is able to witness an ambush or row taking place, all the better. Any mob will have its favourite tactics, and if these can be seen in action it is easier to plan counter-measures.

We have spoken to many scouts who, without exception, and for obvious reasons, wanted to remain anonymous. They all gave vivid and very candid accounts of what they do and why they do it, and although one may have a grudging respect for these men, it is frightening that not one of them showed any regret or remorse for a single thing – and some of these men were responsible, directly or indirectly, for some major incidences of football violence. They were all in fairly respectable employment, which was a good thing for them, because they were, in some cases, spending a great deal of money on watching matches in which they had absolutely no interest. Their motivation was pure love of their team, a belief in what they were doing and a fierce pride in the reputation of their respective firms.

The following reports are fairly typical of the sort of thing we were told and give a chilling insight into the way information is obtained and used, often to devastating effect.

Oxford Away

A few seasons back, I was scouting part-time for my club, one of the big London clubs. We had drawn Oxford away in the Cup, and as the boys hadn't played at the Manor Ground for a couple of years, basically because Oxford are a shitty little second-rate team, I was tasked to pay a visit to suss things out. Now, having the sort of job I do [working for one of the leading high-street banks], it was not difficult to me to find someone I knew at university at Oxford. So on the Friday afternoon I headed up the M40, alone for once, to stay with an old mate who supported another London club.

Anyway, by about eight o'clock we were out on the town pissing it up with all the students and having a whale of a time. As is usual, the talk soon turned to football – or rather, I turned it that way – and I started pumping them for information which, in a room of pissed-up students, was soon pouring into my memory banks. It quickly became apparent that Oxford had a fairly respectable little mob with a hard core of about 100 and a good few cling-ons who could be relied upon in most cases. I quickly learned where the majority of those from Oxford itself met up and where the fans from the outskirts usually congregated prior to coming into the city for a few beers before the game. They had no real organisation among the fans, which was not surprising, really: Second Division club means second-division fans, and if anything went off at all, it was usually on the spur of the moment. Although the local papers were full of us coming in a couple of weeks, the only people starting to worry were the police, who had insisted that the game be made all-ticket. Just what I wanted to hear.

The next morning, after dealing with my hangover, I again turned the conversation to football and found, to my feigned surprise, that Oxford were at home that afternoon. It was not a difficult job to persuade my mate, along with his two student flatmates, to attend, but before this I had to go into town on the pretence of doing a bit of shopping. The team Oxford were playing was just another second-rate club, but by eleven they had a few little mobs of about fifteen or so wandering around the town centre, just front-ing up, I suppose. However, there were no Oxford fans to be seen anywhere, and this started to interest me because usually it means that they are mobbing up somewhere else.

No one should be able to take liberties like that, should they?

I started to follow one of these groups to see what they would get up to and what opposition, if any, they encountered. I was beginning to think that Oxford were total wankers when, just as this group walked past a pub, it all went off. These guys just poured out, steamed in and kicked the shit out of this little mob before they knew what had happened, and then they did the off. As I watched all this, from a respectful distance, of course, I was actually quite impressed because even I, someone who was seriously looking for them, had no idea where they were. Nice one.

From here, I took a stroll out to the station, which in Oxford is on the opposite side of the city centre from the ground. Again, I found no one of any significance other than opposing fans arriving. This was turning out to be pretty weird. It was completely different from what I was used to. But from the number of police around, it was obvious that things were usually quite heavy.

By now, it was time to meet my mates at their favourite haunt and head to the ground. As I walked in I got the shock of my bloody life. Here were their mob – or at least, a large portion of it – and my mates were sat drinking with them. I soon settled in, and after taking the standard 'Cockney wanker' abuse, was quickly accepted and started talking football. I told them I had seen some of their boys in action and they told me that this was one of their usual tactics: everything would happen after the game, because as the support was so spread out around the surrounding areas, they all met up at the stadium and went from there.

As much of this information was contrary to what I had heard the night before, I realised that my assumption that they were almost totally disorganised had been in the main correct, but that what mob they did have were well up for it. It also became clear that they were not looking forward to our lot coming up, because they knew that they would get a hammering, if for no other reason than strength of numbers.

We left for the ground at about 1.30 and arrived just before 2 p.m. The majority of the lot I was with hung around outside until about 2.30 and then went into the home end. Standard stuff, really, and following a staggeringly uninteresting game we poured out of the ground and found all the lads we had met in the pub heading round to the side of the ground to front up the opposing fans as they came out of their end. As usual, the police prevented anything happening in this area and the mobs moved off in their respective directions. By now, I had seen and heard enough. I knew where their mobs drank, roughly how many there were, what time they got to the ground and had a good idea of what they would do if anything went off. This, coupled with the fact that I had seen their little 'hit-and-run' ploy in action, meant that I had all I needed.

When I met up with the lads from my real club on the Wednesday, I passed on the full report. It soon became apparent that because this was a Cup game, the lads wanted to put on a show, something that Oxford would remember, and so I passed on a few ideas that had come to me as I had walked around the city on the Saturday morning. Armed with a map, I pointed out two or three pubs that were worth a visit, but the big one would come at the service station on the ring road north of the city. This was where many of the fans met up before the game, and they would never expect us to go there as it was on the other side of Oxford from London. About fifty or so hard core plus cling-ons would go there, another mob to the railway station and the remainder of the crew would do the pubs, everyone meeting at the ground at about two o'clock. From there, it was into the city centre after the game for the usual piss-up and rampage. It was as simple as that. Once agreed, the plans and travel arrangements were circulated as normal. The only worry was the police presence, which would be very heavy for us, but we knew that if anyone got nicked, they would almost certainly be released after the game or in the morning, just as they almost always were.

That was it, the end of my involvement in that incident. I like to hear about the games I scouted for, but usually all I get are the reports that come back from the front-liners a few days later. However, this time my mate rang me up to tell me that our lads had really gone to town and basically took Oxford over. Everywhere a group of fans had gathered they had been hit. 'It was fucking uncanny,' he said. He had heard that some Oxford lads had tried a 'hit-and-run' from a pub, only to find that what they thought was a small mob was actually only half a crew, with the remainder walking about 20 metres behind. They had steamed out of the pub, run straight into a trap and got the shit done out of them. If only he bloody knew – that's exactly what I had suggested. He also told me that there was a big off at the service station on the ring road, and that his local had been taken over by 'Cockney bastards' who had all but totalled it. All of this was a total surprise to me, of course, and to this day he has no bloody idea, and neither does anyone else. Still, that's why I'm one of the best scouts there is. My information is always spot-on, you see.

Sussed

There are two reasons why I scout. The first is that I like nothing better than planning a raid and then finding out how it all went, and the second is that although I love fighting, I can't fight for bollocks and the only way I could help the lads to 'do the business' was to scout. The downside to this, of course, is that as my family still live in the Midlands I usually scout the Midlands games, which means I never see my own team play away matches near my parents' home. I also have to watch loads of shit games and there is the odd occasion when I get sussed, and that means trouble.

The worst time was when I went to scout at St Andrews as our lads had a game with Birmingham coming up and

wanted to have a bit of a party. I drove up with my mate
and parked not far from the ground at about eleven o'clock.
Within twenty minutes we were firmly established in a pub
with a load of Blues fans. As far as they were concerned, we
were Birmingham fans through and through: we had done
our work and knew all the details of their latest results and
current squad, and the few questions they threw at us were
answered correctly and quickly, as normal. It all started to
go wrong when my mate made the mistake of saying that
he had been involved in a row at a Birmingham game,
because although he had, he described it from the point of
view of the opposition (us), and the kicking 'they' (we)
dealt out to 'us' (Birmingham). Although many of the
blokes we were sat with agreed with everything he said,
thick bastards, a couple of them started to become suspicious and began throwing questions at us about other
games.

When you come from the Midlands but live in the south,
and supposedly still support a team in the Midlands, it is
hard to explain why you are hardly known by anyone and
only ever watch 'your' team play at a certain ground
(ours). The more we tried to explain, the deeper in we got. I
even tried the old 'Well, I haven't really been to many
games. I'm just repeating what someone else said' routine
but these bastards had started to smell a rat, or two. I
realised we were in big, big trouble. Suddenly, one of them
asked us outright: 'Are you two fuckers scouting?'

I just looked at him and said, 'Yes.'

'Who for?'

By now the whole pub was staring at us with a look of
total hatred, and when I told him who we were scouting
for, this look intensified about ten times. I think even the
girl behind the bar would have glassed us given half a
chance. The immortal, and often-mocked phrase, 'Well,
we'd better give you something to talk about, then, you
arsehole,' was the cue for them to go to town on the pair of
us, and we got the hiding of our lives. The bastards even

stole our wallets and keys, which in the end was even worse than getting a hiding. At least my car was all right, although I had to get it broken into by the AA.

All of this, of course, was highly amusing to the lads at home when we passed it on and to this day, if anyone wants to wind me up, 'Brum, Brum!' is more than sufficient. It was even worse when we did play them, because the lads tried to avenge our pasting and took a right bloody hammering from their poxy Zulu Army.

It is one thing to scout, but to be scouted is quite another. If someone is looking at you, it will be for a reason, and almost certainly an unfriendly one. This letter was sent to us by Mark S. from Norfolk.

Meeting Point

Like thousands of other fans from clubs up and down the country, I actually live a few miles away from our local ground, but over the years I've been going, I've met up with loads of lads from my home town and we now start off in a local pub and travel to games together as a crew. What began as a laugh eventually led on to other things, and we quickly became known as a naughty little firm of about thirty blokes, more than capable, and certainly willing, to hold our own anywhere and this was a reputation we were quite happy to live with. Within our crew was possibly the nastiest piece of work I have ever known, the sort of bloke who, when you're in a ruck, is worth his weight in gold because he's a nutter and will pull any stunt to get a result if it goes off. Now, don't get me wrong, like the vast majority of fans he's a great bloke away from football, but at games, Jesus, he scares the shit out of me, and I'm no one's mug. This guy had started to get a serious reputation around other mobs and was well known at England games and all that shit, but he had managed to evade the police so he didn't really live in fear of the dreaded dawn raid like some of us did.

A few seasons ago we had a home game and as usual planned to meet up at our local for a few before making our way to the ground. A few of our lads, including our top boy, wouldn't be there as they were working and were due to meet us at the ground. I arrived at the pub early and I'm stood at the bar with about five or six other lads when these two blokes walk in, order a soft drink and then sit down. To tell you the truth, I didn't think too much about them – they were pretty ordinary, actually. They sat in a corner facing the door and just carried on talking to each other, so we ignored them. As more of our lads came in, the usual supporter's instincts started to make us interested in these blokes. Although they couldn't possibly cause us any grief – numbers alone would ensure that – some of the lads were getting slightly edgy, and a couple were sure that they knew them, but they couldn't work out from where. The landlord was equally puzzled about who they were. He said he was sure they had been in before, but weren't we getting a bit paranoid about two blokes having a drink?

Eventually, one of our lot went over and asked them outright who they were and what they wanted. As we watched, he started laughing and, after a little chat, he walked back over to us. 'They're only fucking salesmen having a drink. They're poxy Rugby League fans, fuck all to care about.' By this time, we needed to leave for the ground, but there was still this doubt about these two blokes and it kept nagging at a few of us right through the game. They weren't what the cockneys would call 'kosher', if you get what I mean.

After the match, we went back to our local and the landlord called me over. 'Those two fellas you were interested in left you this.' He handed me a letter which basically said 'We'll be seeing you wankers.' It meant only one thing: the fuckers had been on a scouting mission and we were a target for someone. The other lads freaked out, they went mental, but no matter what we did there was no way we could find out who they were. We didn't have a single clue. The 'why' didn't matter – in this game you're always a target for some tosser. All we could do now was wait. When our boy found out, he just laughed. 'At last,' he said. 'If we're being scouted, we've made the fucking big time.'

At every game from then on, it was a case of setting someone outside the pub as a lookout in case we were hit, but it just didn't happen, not at the next game, nor the one after that. In the end we got bored with waiting for them, settled back into the routine we had enjoyed before our visit and forgot about what had happened. It was about two months later that they visited us – I'm not saying who they were, because sooner or later we'll reply in kind, but we'll have to go some to beat what they did to us. There were about fifteen of us in the pub when, with no warning at all, almost every window came in, closely followed by what seemed like 100 blokes but what was probably more like twenty.

These guys were well organised and extremely violent. They knew exactly what they were doing and systematically wrecked the pub and us. It was total mayhem and we didn't have a chance, we got totally battered. As they started to pull out, one of them started screaming 'Where's your fucking boy? Where is the wanker then? We thought you'd be up for it, you wankers, but you're just shit!' That was when I knew who they were really after, and the twat wasn't even there. The other thing we quickly realised, especially when we found the calling cards they left us, was that this mob were from a club that were in a different division from us, and so we would never get a chance for revenge because there was no fucking way that we could get a mob together to take to their place, not in a million years.

By this time they had vanished, the pub and us were blitzed and as more of the lads turned up and saw what had happened, they didn't know whether to laugh because they had escaped it all or cry because they had missed it.

The landlord went mental, of course, and banned us all on the spot, and then the idiot called the police, so everyone who could pissed off quick while the rest of us ended up in casualty, which meant that, just to add insult to injury, we missed our game.

When our boy eventually turned up, he saw what had happened and got to the ground as quickly as possible to organise a mob to take quick revenge on our opposition. Someone had to pay. But the coppers were all over the place and well on top of anything and everything near the ground. There was no sign of the scum who had done us over, although we heard on the grapevine later that those who had raided us were one of the firms on the way up. They had raided many groups like ours that season and were, as we thought, after our boy, which, if nothing else, meant that they might well pay us another visit.

After that, a few of the lads started to have second thoughts about what we had got ourselves into. We had really thought that we were a big-time mob and were quite well organised, but the fact that this crew had travelled quite a way just to do us certainly made some of them realise that we were way out of our league. A few of them have stopped going to games altogether now, and I can see their point. It wasn't just the battering that hurt; it was the fact that our reputation as a mob had been destroyed in one single ruck and that our own personal pride had been dented. No one likes to think that anyone can give them a slapping. Even our top boy started to have doubts – not about what happened to us lot, but about whether our mob were good enough for him. He's started to recruit another group of lads for another firm. For myself, well, I have to say that although I still get up to the odd bit of mischief, I'll never get involved with anything like that again. That's way too heavy for me, I'm afraid, and I want none of it.

Another person, similar in status and commitment to the scout, and whose role in organised groups should not be discounted, is the spotter. Spotters deal with the gathering of information on matchday itself and will be hard at work sorting out where and when attacks or ambushes are to take place long before their actual mobs arrive at their destination. At home or away, the spotter's job is to find out how his club's rivals have travelled, how many of them there are, where they are meeting and, more importantly, where they are drinking, because pubs are an obvious target for any attack. He then has to relay that information to the main mob which, these days, with the advent of the relatively cheap mobile phone, is a lot easier than it used to be.

Like the scout, the spotter is usually someone who blends into the crowd, or who travels around by motorbike so that he or she can move quickly and hide behind the mask that a crash helmet provides. Like scouting, spotting is a risky business, because at an away game on unfamiliar territory it is all too easy to get lost and caught, with obvious consequences. Here is a story sent to us by a spotter which shows only too clearly how dangerous an occupation it can be.

The Spotter

About five seasons ago I was heavily involved with the main mob of one of the big First Division clubs and became mixed up in all sorts of stuff which I'm not particularly proud of now. I won't go into how I got into this, because it isn't any different from the way most other people do, I suppose, but for a time I was involved in scouting and spotting, which, if you need an adrenaline rush, is the thing to do.

The first time I ever did any spotting was when we were playing a pre-season game at one of the smaller London clubs. Talk about in at the deep end! Although the club looked upon this game as a friendly, it was certainly not a word that we would have used, because we had got whispers from some of our London supporters' groups that we would be getting a warm welcome from some of the other London firms. It was quickly circulated among the main mob that we were not prepared to put up with a slapping of any kind, and so plans were laid to get as many fans down to London as we possibly could without anyone expecting us.

This meant that any forms of organised travel was out of the question, and while the club itself expected about 2,000 'genuine' fans to be at the game, we quickly established that we would take about seventy lads who were all 'ready for work', as it were. The basic plan was to travel, separately by car, van and train and all meet at King's Cross, where the main group would then wait for any information to come back to them from the three spotters, of which I was one, who would travel down by motorbike and link up with some of the more informed London lads to suss things out during the afternoon.

So the three of us on our bikes arrived in London at about three in the afternoon and met the three lads who would be our passengers for the afternoon outside King's Cross. From there, we parked the bikes and had a quick meal in a burger bar, where we spent about half an hour working out where we would need to go to find the mobs who were looking for us. The general opinion among the three Cockney lads was that we would stand a good chance of seeing their group if we had a look at a few pubs on the North Circular and then went down towards the ground, which is exactly what we did, but with little or no luck. By around 4.30, the six of us had found almost no one to speak of and so we decided to split up and meet back at King's Cross at six o'clock which was about the time the main body of our lot were due to arrive.

Another half-hour later we still had nothing and the lad with me had all but run out of ideas as to where we would need to go next. We even got to the stage where we thought that nothing was going to happen at the game, despite what we had heard on the grapevine, so we thought about getting to King's Cross and just telling the lads to find a pub and have a beer before the game. Just as we were about to give up, the bloke with me spotted a car with a load of lads in it, one of whom was wearing a Spurs T-shirt. We took off after them to find out if they would lead us anywhere. After about twenty minutes, they pulled into a pub where the car park was full of cars and vans and where all these geezers were sat outside drinking. By sheer luck, we had stumbled across a fair-sized mob, and with a tube station about 100 yards away. Here was our target.

We screamed back to King's Cross to find that the other two spotters had drawn a complete blank and so we waited for our lads to turn up on a train which, for once, was early. We soon discovered that all the lads on the train, without exception, were pissed out of their minds following some serious drinking in the buffet car and there was no way, as far as we were concerned, that they would be any good for anything. We went mental, not just because we had wasted our time and money spotting for them, but because we had missed out on a good piss-up ourselves and faced a long ride home after the game. The lads who had driven down were now starting to arrive, and eventually, out of about sixty lads, there were no more than twenty, including us six, who were ready for it. But despite my advice to the contrary, the lads still wanted to ambush the mob we had found – that, after all, was the reason they had come to London. But there was no way they would get anything but a serious hiding, from what we could see of them, and from what we had seen of the other mob. Still, in for a penny and all that. So we told them which tube station to head for and the three of us rode back towards the pub to keep an eye on the London mob from across the road.

When we got there, I was relieved to find that their mob were still drinking heavily, but I was somewhat dismayed to see that their numbers had now swelled to about 100, which was more than enough to sort our lot out in the state they were in. As we watched, they started to drink up and head for the tube and we quickly realised that they would walk right into our mob heading towards them. There was almost nothing we could do, but one of the lads jumped on his bike and shot round to the station to warn our lads what was happening. Although we went after him, we had the sense to stay across the road with our engines running, just in case. Our boy jumped off his bike and ran into the station, but there was no sign of our lot and so he decided to wait for the next train to see if they were on that one.

But by then their crew were coming into the station and down on to the platform. You can guess what happened. The train came in, our lads got off and found that on the opposite platform were about fifty geezers. What they couldn't see were the other fifty walking towards them, so they decided to have a go and ran up to the exit to get down on to the opposite platform. Their mob, seeing ours, did the same and all we could hear across the road was a major off which soon spilled out on to the main road. From our vantage-point, we could see that our lot were not doing too badly, but the reinforcements which were currently heading at full speed down the road quickly ensured that they got the shit kicked out of them. The lad who had gone into the station to warn them managed to get to his bike and was off like Barry Sheene on acid while we sat on our bikes, engines running, watching it all unfold. There was no way we could do anything – there were only two of us left! The police were there within about five minutes, which was a bloody good job for our lot, because they had taken a real hammering. A couple of them ended up in hospital with broken bits.

Of course they all blamed us because we hadn't given them all the information and should have warned them what was going on – as if there was any way we could have. Besides, if they were stupid enough to go looking for a ruck when they were pissed then they got what they deserved, stupid twats.

Chapter 8
The East Enders

It is common knowledge among supporters that there are a number of clubs whose fans have been at the forefront of football violence for many, many years. Indeed, for many supporters, the mere mention of the names of these teams evokes memories of trouble caused throughout the country. Although these clubs can be found all over England, most supporters will acknowledge that two of the most infamous sets of fans are from East London, and they are, of course, West Ham and Millwall. For their part, the clubs themselves have done as much as is possible to eradicate the threat of violence from their grounds, and indeed, Millwall in particular are to be praised for their efforts in forging closer links with both families and the local community. A visit to the original Den was one of the most feared fixtures in football, whereas the New Den is a model stadium with superb facilities which are a credit to everyone concerned, even though it can still be one of the most intimidating places we know. However, as we have attempted to prove, football violence is outside the control of the clubs themselves. At the level we are examining it is a highly organised, well-planned and potentially deadly activity carried out by people who clearly see their role as an extension of the playing staff's attempts to ensure that their team are the best.

Upton Park, the home of 'the Hammers' and terraced cathedral for the footballing East Enders, is the home of the ICF, the Inter-City Firm, probably the most famous footballing mob in the world and renowned for leaving their calling cards with victims. However, most of what is commonly known about this group is myth: stories that have grown up on the terraces, been added to and settled into legend but which, in truth, are utter bollocks. What is true is that the ICF is a huge mob boasting some of the most active hooligans and some of the best organisation of any firm in football. It is also common knowledge that, as is the case in most mobs these days, the bulk of the planning and organisation by the ICF is done using mobile phones and that the majority of the members have good, in some cases very good, careers. For them, violence is a release, the British male's equivalent to what the Americans call 'therapy'. Travel by rail is the norm, hence their name, and they will, and do, go everywhere. The notorious occasion on which one of the cross-Channel ferries was turned back mid-way through its journey due to the behaviour of West Ham fans on board is one of the most revered stories on the terraces. This is not to say, of course, that West Ham supporters themselves escape the threat of attacks by rival gangs – on the contrary, no club with a reputation like theirs can expect to go unchallenged and the famous, or infamous, episode when a pub full of Hammers fans was attacked by a Newcastle mob armed with, among other things, Molotov cocktails and darts, is probably the most widely known example.

West Ham fans have rivals and enemies throughout the country, and every away trip is a potential battleground, a situation that is accepted with relish by many of the travelling faithful. One of the favourite tactics of Hammers fans at away matches is the infiltration of the home end, because this is the area which offers not just the greatest chance of victory, but also the best opportunity to humiliate the home fans. We have seen this ploy in action many times at Vicarage Road, and while many clubs, ours included, use it, with West Ham in particular it is the numbers involved that cause the problems. One Chelsea supporter gave us an account of a time when Hammers fans infiltrated the Shed wearing not only blue and white scarves, but in some cases Chelsea shirts as well. Before and during the first half, Chelsea groups had attacked the Hammers supporters in the away end, but as nothing had gone off in the Shed, they believed that West Ham had bottled it. At half-time, all pretence was dropped and West Ham fans appeared at every point on the terrace and went berserk. It was only staggering defence by the Blues fans, as well as sterling work by the police, that prevented them from taking the end and claiming what for them would have been a momentous victory. The same thing has been tried at many grounds, and Highbury seems to be a favourite target.

For almost every First Division club, Millwall away is one of the most dreaded fixtures of the season, as we have mentioned. The very name Millwall has a thuggish ring to it, and although it is still feared it has suffered more than most from the legions of armchair teenage fans and trendies who wear Millwall shirts because they want to look hard, but who would never dream of actually visiting East London. What still holds true, however, is the reputation of a number of this club's followers as one of the most violent groups of supporters in existence. Moreover, the original Millwall mob, the F–Troop, who used to wear some very strange headgear, remain possibly the most feared firm ever seen at an English football ground. When Millwall visit your home ground, it is almost inevitable that something will happen somewhere, because it seems as if some of their supporters feel duty-bound to create problems.

Possibly the most widely known incident involving Millwall fans was the episode at L*t*n, when the ground was overrun and wrecked, something that was seen throughout the footballing world. It was almost certainly because of this one incident that the organisation of football violence became widely acknowledged and accepted. This was no spur-of-the-moment fight, it was premeditated violence on a scale rarely seen inside stadiums, even in those days. This was the riot that led the police to take even tougher action to remove the problem of hooliganism from within football grounds. We have been told of many other incidents involving Millwall fans, including the infamous battle when West Ham fans were ambushed at Surrey Quays railway station by a group of Lions fans armed with pit-bull terriers, which were promptly released and caused havoc among their hated rivals. However, an account we were given is one of the most sinister we have ever come across because the violence was so well planned, right down to the last detail, and could have been absolutely deadly if the fans themselves had not exercised restraint.

The Trap

We were in our first season back down and all year we had been going to town because at every game people were giving it the big 'un, which was pissing us off. So what do you do? Too right, go mad and do the bastards. We had been everywhere with the boys, even the pre-seasons, and had got ourselves into some right scalps. I remember when we played Barnsley, I think, some of the lads rolled one of their vans on to its side just for a laugh and then hung around to see their faces when they got back. That was the first year I actually went to court rather than being let off with a warning or something. The bastards put me on community service or some such shit. Fuck that for a laugh – there was no way I was going to miss the lads playing just to do some old bag's garden. Anyway, everyone who came to the Den bottled it. They were all total wankers; not one of them had tried anything all season. A few of them had gone for it when we were away, but only one of them had got anywhere with us, and that was Bristol City. A load of our lads had been in a pub when their mob came in and turned them over. One of my mates was put in hospital by some bastard with a blade and because of this, we planned something for them that we had been saving up for ages. We had to show these wankers that there was no way they were going to be allowed to go around telling everyone that they had done Millwall. We knew that they would bring a lot down because they were going well, and all these tossers like to say that they've been to Millwall and turned us over. Total bollocks, of course, but there you are.

Our plan had been kicking around for years, one of those things that come about when you're travelling. But this time we were going to do it. The first thing we had to do was to find out how many they were bringing down and how many of them were coming on coaches. A quick call to their travel office and we knew that were about six or seven coaches, which company they used and that the rest of their fans were arriving by train. This stupid cow in their office would have told us anything we wanted: she didn't even ask who we were or anything, just gave us all this stuff and helped us on our way – perfect. We then contacted the coach company, who happily told us the route they would be taking – somehow they got the idea that we were from the police or something – and that was it, all we needed.

On the Saturday, the coach drivers from Bristol were making their way to our place when they came across some road signs directing all football coaches to hang a left at the next turning. What they did not and could not know was that they were heading directly into a dead end and this was an ambush. Down this side street were about 150 Millwall who were, without exception, tooled up and hyped up. When the coaches drove down and came to a stop we steamed out and let them have it – bricks, bottles, the full bollocks – and every window on every bus went through. I tell you, it was total fucking mayhem, and they were shitting it because not one person tried to get off any of the coaches and have a go back. We then followed this up by steaming on to the coaches which held anything we thought resembled a mob and beating the shit out of them with fists and sawn-off broom handles, which can really do the bollocks to people and are easily hidden or thrown away. Hardly anyone tried to have a go back, the only ones who did were the coach drivers, and they were dealt with quite easily, poor bastards. This whole thing was amazing.

We planned and did it all perfectly. Within about five minutes we had totally fucked up six coaches and everyone on board and then we did the off. I actually stopped about 100 yards away and looked back, and still no one had got off. I almost felt sorry for them. The Filth came to see where they were and found a scrapyard and a bloody casualty ward, and there was nothing they could do about it. I tell you what, though, they were bloody quiet during the game, and have behaved themselves ever since. That's what we like, a bit of respect. We deserve it from wankers like that. Millwall are the best there is. No one likes us, we don't care.

As you have just read, the defence of home territory is paramount to all of those who take part in violence at football and they will go to almost any length to ensure that no liberties are taken by visiting supporters. Travelling away, however, is a completely different ball game.

PART FOUR
Away Days

Chapter 9
Travel

For many supporters, one of the greatest attractions of football is that it gives you the chance to travel the country, visit other grounds and meet new people. For the genuine fan, this is a wonderful thing indeed as it broadens the horizons as well as giving a good insight into how good or crap your own ground is, depending on which team you support. It is, of course, also a great feeling to go to an opposition stadium and watch your lads turn someone over, and I'm sure that simply reading this sentence will bring back some great memories of last-second winners out of nowhere and so on. It is all well and good to visit places like Plymouth and Hartlepool, if you like that sort of thing, but let's be honest, the reason that some people travel is that they get the chance to hurl abuse at (and possibly ruck with) supporters from other parts of England. Speaking for the majority of southerners, there is no doubt at all that we get a great deal of pleasure from taking the piss out of our northern cousins, and we know that exactly the same thing applies in reverse. Even when the recession of the late eighties and early nineties turned the country on its head, up north we southerners still did what we do best: put on a show of cockiness and arrogance in that excellent Mike Baldwin-type way. The northerners, of course, do their best to wind us up (usually with something like 'Up the apples an' pears, guv'nor') but it never really works because we know that they do not really believe in their jibes like we do in ours. Remember Harry Enfield's creation Loadsamoney? He was a great bloke, the best weapon we ever had. A good few seasons ago, when the south was at its most prosperous, a lot of we Watford supporters went to Wembley to watch the FA Trophy final, which happened to be being played by two northern teams, the object being, for once, merely to watch a game of football, nothing else. Eddy, the co-writer of this book, however, had different ideas. While we were queuing to get in, he launched into an extremely loud 'Poor northerners/ the pits/Scargill' monologue and boasted that he earned as much in a week as they did in a month. The crowning glory of his performance, which became the focus of attention of everyone within 30 feet, was when he pulled out his wallet and said to the rest of us: 'I know! We're all loaded, so why don't we pay for all these northerners to get in?' With a perfect comedian's pause that Bob Monkhouse would have paid for, he added, 'No, fuck 'em!' The whole place erupted into laughter.

Travelling, of course, also gives you the right – no, the duty – to abuse everyone else from your club who did not travel to support the team they claim to worship (some Premier League supporters, obviously, cannot help it as they cannot get tickets even for home games never mind away ones). There will be plenty of people among this number who will claim that they did actually travel but 'sat in the stands with a friend from the area', but we know that they are lying. With these lies comes the risk that they will be found out and abused even more.

The majority of 'normal' fans have, over the seasons, earned our respect for dealing with ill-treatment and crap conditions at away matches, not to mention expensive club-run travel schemes. The people we are concerned with here, however, would not be seen dead on a supporters' coach, or any club-endorsed trip, for that matter. They are the travelling mobs. These groups do not really give a toss about the other supporters; indeed, they view them as intruders into their own, totally separate, game, in which the match itself is sometimes of secondary importance to the battle for a result in another arena.

Travel

In the whole of the debate on football violence, if there is one area which proves conclusively that a great deal of it is pre-planned, then it is the travelling groups. To get even fifty people to meet up at a set time and then travel to a match together is quite a task (and a bloody expensive one, at that). It has, over the years, become progressively easier to move quickly and safely across the country, with the result that the mobs are able to travel with relative speed and anonymity, which are both in themselves good weapons. Many firms have become quite crafty in their transport arrangements in their attempts, usually successful, to surprise both the police and their potential targets. For example, we know of at least two separate mobs who own their own removal-type lorry. They drive it to the target town, pull up right outside a pub containing opposing supporters, drop the back and disgorge their passengers to cause maximum trouble before anyone realises what is happening.

The mobs' more usual modes of transport are a coach (hired from a different company from the one used by their club, of course). The trouble here is that the coach drivers occasionally take offence at instructions which include a riot stop-off at a particular town; a hired minibus (limits you to a maximum of fifteen blokes); cars (again hired – would you take your own if you knew it might get totalled?) which are limited to a maximum of five; and finally the train. Despite the ridiculous costs involved (although in the past not many of the group actually paid), British Rail have always provided the best method of travel if there are plenty of you, and on most services will even provide you with somewhere to eat and drink. What more could you ask? A few years ago, when the old-fashioned carriages were used, they even provided a source of weaponry for those so inclined, as the many wrecked trains proved. The Inter-City trains, and the tubes come to that, supplied in themselves a moving arena for some horrifically violent encounters between supporters travelling to different games, especially on trains travelling north, as the Cockney Reds would almost certainly come into contact with some rival group or other.

The very fact that travel is so easy makes it simple for supporters to stop off and hit towns en route, something which has happened all over the country for years. In the north, it is well known that many groups travel to games by rail but get off for 'refreshments' a couple of stops before their destination. This inevitably leads to the odd encounter which, as the police have so little notice, can quickly escalate into something far more serious. A few years ago it was common knowledge in our home town that if Everton were playing down south, the fans coming by road would stop off at a particular pub on the way back. This, of course, led to some massive fights with local groups from other clubs until the police finally realised what was happening. Similarly, back in the early eighties, Birmingham at Watford meant running battles at almost every station between the two grounds as they are on the same railway line.

On the roads, meanwhile, the motorway network has enabled many firms to carry out the infamous ambushes and hit-and-runs because they can be in and out of a town within minutes, certainly before the police are aware of anything happening. In fact many mobs will leave and then return to the target pub or club about four hours later, when nobody, least of all the police, is expecting anything. The service stations, which previously welcomed football coaches with about as much warmth as they would a convoy of new-age travellers, now provide excellent meeting points for groups of supporters travelling to games, including those planning any sort of activity. As we have seen, the mobile phone is now used to circulate information around the firm; it also enables members of a mob to split up, travel separately and meet up somewhere later.

In the past, service stations were scary places to visit on matchdays because you never knew what or who you would meet. For some reason things are different nowadays. If we stop at a Welcome Break full of supporters from other clubs, we just want to talk to them, and, usually, they want to talk to us, which is great. However, that is often where the mobs get much of their intelligence from. It used to be the case that London clubs would never fight each other outside London but would either play football on the grass or join up to fight the northerners, but it is rare to hear of anything like that today.

One of the major drawbacks of being a travelling fan is the weather, because you never know what it will be like when you arrive at your destination. During the winter months games often have to be postponed, and if you're already travelling, what do you do? You get out the paper and find another match to go to, which, now that most big games are all-ticket, means a lower division match. This, of course, causes the locals huge problems. They suddenly find themselves saddled with an extra, and totally unexpected, crowd of blokes which, if they are a busy mob, can be real trouble. Worse still, rival groups from the cancelled game, or even two mobs from different grounds, might choose to move on to the same match. Many years ago, we went to watch Watford play at York. It was snowing all the way up, and we half expected the game to be cancelled. Thankfully, it was not, but we were joined on the open terraces by mobs from both Bradford and Rotherham, whose matches were off. It was total mayhem. The police were totally lost because they were faced not only with twice the numbers they had expected, but with a crowd which was comprised almost entirely of lads up for trouble.

Apart from the weather, the other main problem when travelling is the police. If you travel by train, you meet them quite quickly, but if you go by road, you can be outside the ground before they appear. Sometimes, you meet them as you leave the nearest motorway when they may well stop you and give you directions (and not just how to get to the ground!). The problems for, and with, the police are covered elsewhere in this book, but it does seem to us that they are sometimes too quick to condemn all fans as hooligans, which does not endear them to the supporters who aren't looking for trouble.

So there you are, walking out of the station or coach park, fifty strong and fully pumped up and ready to go, the law are across the road and busy talking into their chests and the buzz is so loud it's deafening. What comes next? Loads of singing and tons of noise – you can't beat it. You try to intimidate the locals to let them know that you have arrived. It is all part and parcel of being a fan. The search for a pub that will admit you is usually the next step and, these days, the police will guide you to one that has been suitably 'advised'. There, the much-touted perception of the football fan as a drunken yob will receive a huge boost in the run-up to kick-off.

If you manage to survive the pub – that is, if it hasn't been hit – the time will come when you need to get to the ground. The police, who will have been keeping an eye on the group, will usually escort you to the ground. This obviously gives you another chance to make yet more noise to further intimidate the home supporters before you are finally shown into the ground. Following the game, you will inevitably be kept in for however long the police want, after which you will be escorted back to your waiting trains or buses by the police and shadowed by a few local 'heroes' who know that they're safe from attack.

However, the type of fan we are interested in isn't content with a few roudy pints in a pub and some chanting at the opposition. For the travelling mob, the objectives used to be quite clear: cause as much trouble as possible in the town and/or take their end which, as we have stated, means humiliation for the home side and total victory for the visitors. Apart from the odd cases where the visiting fans have gone across the pitch to take an end (as opposed to getting on the pitch to cause mayhem), the only way in is infiltration which is a bloody dangerous game. These days, infiltration is so rare that anyone who does try it is going to land in serious trouble, either from the home fans or the police, or both. In the past, however, if you managed to make it past the stewards and police outside, you then faced the problem of what to do inside. If you mobbed up, you immediately stood out like sore thumbs and were attacked by the home fans. If you stayed apart until a pre-arranged signal, such as a goal, you faced the prospect of someone walking over to ask you what the time was. This method was, and remains, the best way to find out where someone is from. The fact that the person asking you was backed up by a great many other people wanting to know the time did little for your confidence and your only possible tactic was to kick things off there and then if you had any sense at all (in which case, why were you there?).

These days, things are different, due to the change in the stadium environment, and so the mobs tend to target the pubs. We have looked at scouting and spotting already, but that is obviously not the only way in which the home mob's pub can be found, because over the years most of them will be widely known. However, the ways in which they can be hit are varied and the methods are sometimes ingenious, as some of the accounts in this book reveal. We have been told of mobs getting in through every possible way, doors, windows, even up through the cellar, but the one that stands out for us involved a certain mob we know who were in their home pub when the phone rang. When the barman answered, he called for quiet, held the phone out and said: 'I don't know who this is, but he says it's for all of you' at which point the place exploded as the opposing mob flooded in. Perfect timing!

For many fans, a visit to London is an excuse for a party. But one of the great fears is the underground. The tale sent in by J.F., an Ipswich supporter, shows why such fears are well founded.

The Tube

About six years ago now, we were playing at Spurs and about fifty of us had travelled down by train the night before to have a piss-up in Soho and see a few of the sights. As it was early in the season it was still pretty warm, so we all slept outside in Trafalgar Square – well, we tried to sleep through the endless singing and boozing that always happens when we go on away days. We even met up with a load of Everton fans, who were all right until they got pissed – then they turned into the usual Scouse wankers we all know and hate. In the morning, we dived into a McDonald's for one of their breakfasts and a few gallons of coffee and decided to make our way to North London to find a pub for a few beers and a singsong before the game.

As we travelled on the tube, we met the usual little bands of supporters going to watch games and although there were a lot of us, it was all good-natured, with a few laughs, especially with a group of Orient fans – Christ, if you support a club like that, you suffer enough. Anyway, we pulled into this tube station – fuck knows what or where it was – and the place was crawling with West Ham. There were hundreds of them, and they saw us before the train had stopped. The second the doors opened, the bastards were on and they came for us with all guns blazing. This bastard came at me with total hate in his eyes; he flew over the seats, grabbed me and before I could respond pounded my head off the window and then went on to do someone else.

Now, we're no angels and have certainly been around when you talk about trouble at football, but this lot were mad, raving bloody mad, and we were scared shitless. Suddenly, the doors of the train closed and trapped about fifteen of their lot in with us. Boy, did the tables turn. We kicked the shit out of them, I mean big-style: knee-stamping, bollock-booting, the lot. They were hurt and hurt bad, but the strange thing about it was that the train didn't move and all the other bastards outside just had to watch while we did their mates. Well, watch isn't the right word, because they were going mental and trying to beat their way into the train, which still did not move. Then what happens? The fucking doors open again and they pour in. This time the bloody knives are out and they were out of it; they had totally lost it, you could see it in their eyes.

I've often heard it said, but this time we really were fighting for our lives, and we were going crazy. We seemed to drive them out when the doors shut again, but they had dragged a couple of our mates out and they were on the platform while we were stuck on the train, which still didn't bloody move. Our mates were not only getting a kicking, they were getting cut up and we were in a total frenzy trying to get out to stop it. Christ, I've never seen anyone take as much as those lads took. It was bloody horrific and I still don't understand how people can do that sort of thing to someone else. They even held one of them up against the window so that we could see his face as they were kicking him in the back. We were going mental stuck in this train.

The bloody doors opened again and we were out at them like greyhounds, but within seconds, they just disappeared. Even those we had hurt – and there were a few, believe me – had just vanished off the platform. I'm certainly not saying they ran, because mobs like those do not run from anybody or anything. Perhaps they had another appointment, I don't know, but I have never seen anything like that before or since and I hope I never will. I learned two lessons that day and have stuck to them both religiously ever since. I never have or never will travel on the underground again, and I will never go to watch my lads at Upton Park. That mob put me off for life. The way they attacked and the way they vanished was plain scary.

If you talk to any supporter about travelling, he will invariably begin with the best day out he ever had. For a great many people, especially males, it will involve a victory of his own, but not all trips go according to plan. The next two accounts, relayed to us by fellow Watford supporters, are two such examples and say everything there is to say about road trips.

Coventry

The day started as most Saturdays did then. We met down at the local for a few early beers before getting the bus up the M1. In those days, we didn't travel with the supporters' club. We usually hired a coach from a local firm, which nearly always sent us the same driver. He happened to be a fan of our club, so he was made up. He was also not averse to stopping for a beer on the way if we wanted to, which, if nothing else, ensured that his tips would be up! However, on this occasion, the driver the coach company sent had no interest in football whatsoever and it was all we could do to get him to put the sport on the bloody radio.

For once the bus wasn't full – there were only about thirty-two of us making the journey, but it was a good reliable mob so we had no worries. The trip up was the usual mixture of laughs punctuated with beer-drinking and piss stops, which upset our driver no end. Fuck him, we were paying! Due to the stops and our crap driver, who got lost, we arrived in the coach park late so it was straight to the ground for us – at City, it is only about a five-minute walk. We didn't really know much about Coventry City. We had played them a couple of years earlier in a League Cup tie, and I remember that a guy lost an eye during an off in a car park. But we weren't expecting anything serious, because on all our travels, we had never heard anything bad about them.

For me, the walk to the ground is the best part of any away day: the singing, the front, loads of people buzzing around eyeing us up. It's fucking great and never fails to get the old adrenaline pumping. We were mobbed up, watching each other's backs and making loads of noise and they didn't want to know. As we arrived at the ground later than everybody else, the police put our mob down in the lower tier of the stand, all on our own. The rest of our lot were up in the main stand behind us. What surprised us most was that there was no segregation where we were, and right next to us was a little mob of about thirty City fans who were none too pleased at our arrival. There we were, pissed up, mobbed up and in with the enemy. It was Christmas and Easter rolled into one – or so it seemed.

During the game we played up as much as we could without upsetting the Bill too much. Most clubs in those days thought of us as easy pickings – until they were face to face with us, and then they quickly learned the truth. We played on it as much as we could. We sang long and loud, 'Clap your hands, stamp your feet, we are the family club!' over and over, and you could see the faces of the City fans trying to work out if we were total wankers or total nutters. As we sang, their mob gathered until we were well outnumbered and they were looking mighty ugly and mighty pleased that we had been delivered to them on a plate. By now, stories were coming back to us about slaps being dished out in the toilets and tea bars, and there were also a few slaps and lots of verbal being exchanged out in the open. The Bill were starting to take a great deal of interest in us, as some of the lads had started giving one of them a bit of verbal. Christmas and Easter were turning into Hallowe'en, and quickly.

When the game finished – we won 1–0 of course, and the lads took the piss – all the City were taken out by the Bill and we were kept in, as usual. By now, the beer had started to wear off and some of the bottle was starting to go as well, but bollocks, we had got a result and were mighty pleased with ourselves. However, we soon realised that the police had other plans for our little crew as we were not allowed to use the same exit as the rest of the away fans. Instead we were led out around the pitch, behind one of the goals and over to another exit in the corner opposite from where we had been sitting. They took us down the steps, opened the gates and threw us out into the street, closing the gates behind us with one of those thuds you get in old Dracula movies.

We realised that we were on the road back to the coach park, but that our way was blocked by their entire mob – not just the lot who had been with us, but also the blokes from behind the goal. It seemed to me as though the coppers had set us up for a real hammering and had vanished to let them get on with it. The City mob looked as surprised as we were. I think they thought we had come after them, but when a couple of our lads tried to climb back over the gates to escape, it sort of gave the game away. However, they quickly got back into line after a few threats from the rest of us. As we looked at them across the road, the City fans began to realise what was going on and a couple of them were starting to look for it. There was only one way out and that was to front it, and as a guy stepped out and shouted, 'Come on then, you Cockney cunts,' we just moved forward and went for it with fists and boots flying and it really kicked off.

A couple of their lads were thrown straight back into the gardens opposite and we went over the fences like Red Rum on heat. They bottled it. We ran them up the hill and then turned to go back to the coach park while we were still on top, but the rest of their mob had regrouped and now stood directly between us and our destination. Again, there was only one thing to do: we couldn't wait for them to come at us so we ran at them, but this time a lot of them stood firm. It was a case of fighting our way through, which we achieved with feet, fists, anything we had. Although a couple of our lot took a few, we made it through relatively unscathed. By now we were really buzzing, and a few of our lot got carried away and even chased some of their mob who had run down a side street. They got a bit of a pasting, which was only to be expected, dozy twats. When they turned up at the coach park they were still full of it, so all in all, it had been a result. There really is nothing like the feeling of taking on a mob on their home ground.

As we gathered in the coach park with all the other coach loads, a small group of City fans got up on to the railway beside us and started lobbing stones down at the buses, with obvious results. The heavy fences stopped us from getting through but we returned enough fire for them to get the message and they soon fucked off as well, leaving us even happier and the coach drivers highly pissed off. So there you have it. To the City fans we ran – twice: fuck you – and, by the way, we ain't no Cockneys.

Brighton

Saturday and Brighton away, what more could you ask? Well, quite a lot actually, because it was November, bloody freezing and the shops on the seafront were closed. But this was the first time I had ever been to the Goldstone Ground, and I was determined to enjoy it. For that reason I had driven down early to get some decent fish and chips in my face for my dinner. We had a few pints in a nice pub in the centre and got into the ground with no trouble at all before it started to piss down with rain. At that time – it may be the same now – the visitors were on the side and out in the open. We were getting wet through, which is not what you want when you've got a long way to go home, but the lads were really going to town with them and by half-time, we were 3–0 up and coasting. They were crap and we were having a gas – it was fucking great, the perfect day out.

With the players off for a hard-earned cuppa, we started to look around at the opposition wankers, who were about 20 feet away with a fenced-off area separating the two groups. We had already been giving them the biggie all through the first half, and, fair play to them, they had kept at it with us. But now we were looking for specific targets, and this out-standing couple soon came to our attention. This bloke was stood with his bird. He looked a real twat, she looked a real slag – the perfect combination. We gave her so much shit it was embarrassing. We called her anything and everything we could think of just to wind him up, and although she was attempting to ignore us, she was getting a bit upset. He, on the other hand, was going fucking mental, which made it all the better for us, of course. The more we laughed and took the piss, the worse this tosser got. When the players came back out, we tired of shouting at her quite quickly, but this bloke was still going nuts and so every so often we would start on her again just to keep him at it.

Near the end of the game, which we won more than handsomely, they announced the usual shit of keeping us in the ground until their lot had left. Bollocks to this, we thought, and a couple of us shot up to the back as the final whistle went and just made it through some gates, which shut behind us with a resounding thump. We were sud-denly alone and, to our horror, who should be standing across the road with about twenty of his mates? The wanker and his bird! 'Oh shit,' I remember thinking, 'This is it!' We honestly thought that we were going to die, a situation that was not helped when someone pointed at us and screamed: 'There's two of the cunts!'

Faced with this horrific situation, there was only one thing we could do. We walked out into the road shouting, 'Come on then, wankers!' while adopting the usual arms-out-to-the-side, palms-up pose so beloved of football fans. They were quite shocked by this, and actually moved back about 3 feet, which made me think that we might just be able to do a runner down the middle of the road. But at that moment the gates behind us opened and the rest of our lot poured out. At this, this little mob ran at us, but veered off towards the main body of fans coming out of the gates and it really started to go off big-time. 'Fuck me!' I said. 'Let's get the fuck out of here!' We turned and ran like mad down the road in the general direction of where we were parked, laughing our bollocks off. We just could not believe we had got away with it.

When we found the car, we had a quick smoke and then discovered that the poxy thing wouldn't start because of the damp or something. There was no way I was going to get out and start digging around under the bonnet, so we just sat in the car, waiting and listening to the radio, as you do on Saturdays. After about ten of the longest minutes of my life, the inevitable happened and their mob came round the corner and started walking towards us. We quickly dived between the seats and just hid. We had almost got away with it when my mate had to stick his bloody head up to see what was going on and they spotted him. With a yell of triumph they came over, and before we could get out, pushed against the doors to trap us inside. They were bloody delirious: not only had they caught two of the opposing fans, but the two in question were the ones that had been giving them the big 'un all afternoon. This was their chance to avenge all the verbal, as well as the spanking they had just received from the rest of our lot. All I could do was pump the horn in the vain hope that a policeman would arrive and rescue me.

Some bloody hope. Within seconds the bastards were all over the car and it was bloody wrecked. The worst thing of all was that they kept us trapped inside and, just as the police finally arrived, ran off before we could do anything. When I explained what had happened – leaving out the bits incriminating us, of course – the pigs found it difficult to keep from laughing. They thought it was hilarious, the bastards. To add insult to injury, the poxy car started when one of them tried it. I felt a total prick driving home in a car which had every panel, including the roof, kicked in, but not half as stupid as I felt when I had to hand it back to the hire company the next day. Were they pissed or what!

The next three reports, sent to us by fans from various clubs, highlight a few of the more unusual things the travelling fan occasionally has to put up with on his journeys.

Wigan Bridge

This is just a quickie, but even now, after all these years, it cracks me up to think of it. We were on a special going to Bolton for a midweek League Cup game, and all the way up it had been one battle after another. Not with other clubs or anything like that – I'm talking about the ambushes and stuff we carried out on the specials themselves. In those days, British Rail, bless 'em, always gave us the old-style carriages, which meant that all the blokes in each compartment would spend the whole of the trip attacking or being attacked by blokes in other compartments. Nothing serious – well, most of the time it wasn't, anyway – but a great laugh and a great way to kill the time. We were always up to something or other. Once, on a trip to Ipswich, we tied this bloke to the luggage rack and left the little twat there while we went to the game. As you can imagine, he was not a happy geezer when we got back, especially as he'd been left upside down for most of the time. Fuck me, he had the reddest face I have ever seen!

Anyway, to get back to the point, during the journey we had been doing the usual fan-spotting and floodlight-watching stuff and were starting to get apprehensive about the game, something that was brought on by our experience of previous visits to Bolton and trouble with their supporters. As usual, when we got near Wigan station the train began to slow down, and we all started moaning. Trains always stopped for ages at Wigan in those days, but no one ever bothered to tell us why. This time we had stopped on the bridge overlooking the main high street rather than in the station itself. Of course, we all jumped up to start slinging abuse at the poor northerners doing their shopping, but when we stuck our heads out of the window, we saw the most beautiful sight.

Down below us were about 300 or 400 Man City fans, who were being held by the police before being escorted to Springfield Park to see their game with Wigan. We started giving them loads of verbal and they gave us loads back. Then someone lobbed a few toilet rolls, which pissed them off a bit. Next one of our lot grabbed a lightbulb from its socket and threw that down on them. It was closely followed by almost every bulb on the train, and then by all the metal rods from the bottom of the window blinds as well. They went totally mental and were running in every direction to avoid the shower. The coppers were freaked because they didn't know what to do either, but they were soon occupied in stopping them coming back up into the station to get to us. The best thing for us, of course, was that we knew that these wankers couldn't have a go back and we had a great view of them going mad and rucking with the police.

For once the train started again quite quickly and so the police had no time to pull us off, although I think they were a bit busy controlling the Mancs to worry about us in any case. I really hope that some of them will read this just to let them know that whenever I see a City fan, I still have a little chuckle at what we did to them that night and got away with.

The following account, sent to us by Andy from Birmingham, illustrates just how much trouble even a fairly small mob can cause.

Villa

I used to belong to a nasty little firm of lads who watched the Villa, home and away. I ain't too proud to say that we were all more than capable of holding our own against anybody. All told, I suppose there were about twenty of us and at most games there were about fifteen or so – some of us did shift work and couldn't always get to matches. We used to get up to all sorts of stuff; it didn't matter what the other club was, if we could get a result then we would. We tried to stay away from the main Villa mobs as the police were all over them, and we never travelled with any organised group so that we could stop where we wanted. We always hired a van from a place where one of the lads worked, which meant that the back used to be packed out with the lads who all drank like fishes, especially if we were travelling a long way. It also meant that if we stopped anywhere, those in the front could start something off and if anything happened, the back doors would fly open and the cavalry would pour out. I've seen some lads shit themselves when those doors have flown open. It's just a classic ambush and they are well shagged.

One of our favourite tricks was to swap the number plates so that we could get right in and cause some real damage without any chance of the Filth tracing the van back to us. I know it was a bit risky, in case we had an accident or got pulled for something, but it wasn't as if we were going on a picnic anyway. We used to get up to some right stuff then, pulling up outside pubs and putting the windows in, all that sort of thing, but some of the best rucks actually happened during the journey, at service stations and places like that. There's one especially that stands out from the rest because it was just such a great result.

We had just played at Forest, and although there had been a bit of mischief on the way, it had been quite a quiet day for us, really, and we hadn't heard that much about anything happening elsewhere, either. The team were shit and lost, but as most of us were pretty pissed by this time we didn't really care that much. After about half an hour of driving around we left the city to head back to Birmingham. We were bombing along when the traffic slowed down and stopped at this set of lights. Suddenly one of the lads in the front shouted that there was a minibus full of Forest behind us and it was then that we decided to do them, sort of revenge for some trouble we had been in the year before. When the lights changed, the lad driving our van started to edge forward really slowly so that he was at the front of the queue when the lights went orange. He stopped, and everyone behind us was going mad and blaring their horns and all that. My mate got out and started shouting at them all to 'fuck off'.

As you can imagine, the sight of a Villa fan giving all this lot abuse started some of them off, and the driver got out of the minibus and gave him some verbal back. The second he moved away from the door of his van we were out. One of the lads took the driver, and he was on the deck before he knew what was happening. I ran round, pulled the keys out of the ignition and threw them across the road before joining all the other lads in taking on this lot, who by now were screaming out of this bus to get round to us. One of the lads kicked the door back, catching one of them in the face with an almighty whack. He went down like a sack. After a couple of slaps were dealt out to the others, most of them did a runner – no bottle, you see.

We now had a completely blocked main road and a van which couldn't move, and from the look of the people in

the cars behind there was no chance of anyone else getting
out to have a go, so we were in the clear. All we could do
then was to total the bus, and within seconds the windows
and lights were in and the tyres were slashed. Then we
dived into our own van and got the fuck away from there.
As soon as we were a decent distance away, we stopped
and switched the plates back. We thrashed it back to the
motorway and we were away. The Filth didn't even see us,
the tossers.

This account illustrates the problems that ordinary members of
the public can face if they find themselves in the wrong place at
the wrong time. Although most fights take place between rival
gangs, often both looking for action, this sort of situation affects
others.

Euston Station

As any footy fan knows, travelling into and across London
for an away match always get the adrenaline going, and it
all starts when the train pulls into the mainline station you
use. For us, it's Euston. You can guarantee that you will
come across little mobs hanging around at Euston from
most of the London clubs, particularly from those waiting
to pick up on their own opposition, but once you get down
into the tube network, that's when the fun really starts. It's
bloody scary, but the buzz is fantastic. One of the things
you quickly learn about the tube is that it's a bloody dodgy
place to be. When you arrive at a station, a mob of fifty to a
hundred geezers, all well charged up and ready for it, can
just appear out of nowhere and you soon discover that it is
not a good idea to wear colours or make a lot of noise when
you're down there. I speak from bitter experience. I've seen
a lot of digs given out to tossers on the tube, and they're
mainly blokes who are fresh into London, usually for the
first time, and giving verbal to mums and dads, that sort of
thing, people who don't give a shit about them anyway. I

hate to think of some of the things that have gone on down there. But when we've come across one of the larger mobs, such as West Ham or Chelsea, it's always struck me that they are usually so focused on a particular target that they will either ignore you or just give you a load of verbal rather than get involved in anything.

A few years ago we had a game down at Fulham. It went off without any trouble, although we had been expecting a bit of a row from Chelsea, because we had a thing with them due to something that had happened a few years previously. So on the way back to Euston we gathered together a little mob of about fifteen just to look out for each other. We expected most of the other mobs to have gone by the time we got to the station as it always takes a long time to get back from Putney Bridge. But when we came up the escalator we saw loads of little groups hanging around, obviously intent on something. This was not what we expected or wanted to see at all. As we came out all eyes turned towards us and things went quiet, just like they do when you walk into the wrong pub – you know what it's like. After gathering all the front we could muster, we walked straight across the concourse towards our platform. On the way a couple of blokes walked over and asked us how we were, you know the tactic. To our relief, it turned out they were all Arsenal fans checking us out to see if we were Liverpool, so they left us alone.

They had been playing the Scousers at Highbury, and something must have gone off because it was obvious that this lot were waiting to pick off the odd mob getting a train back north. As we looked up at the departures board, we saw that there were a couple of specials waiting for them, which meant that at any time now there was going to be between 400 and 800 Scousers coming through. As there were only about eighty Gunners, this was going to be some off. After a quick chat among the lads we decided to hang around for a while and have a little go ourselves as we hate the wankers as well. If nothing else, we were expecting a giggle.

Suddenly loads of coppers came into the station ready for the arrival of the Scousers and we could hear singing coming from up the tube. All the Gunners started to gather together and the Old Bill saw that they were about to have a major problem on their hands. Can you imagine what the noise was like inside Euston? They were singing their hearts out as they came up the escalator and when the lads at the front realised there was a reception committee waiting for them they spread the word back down. The coppers, for some reason, decided to hold them back rather than move the Gunners, but they just kept coming and coming and the police just didn't have the numbers to deal with them. The Gunners started to front it up, and I must admit that they had more bottle than us, because we held back. But the Scousers just kept appearing out of the tube and they started to realise that they had a much larger mob than Arsenal.

It soon became clear to the Gunners that they were suddenly totally outnumbered and you could see their bottle going, one by one. The Scousers suddenly went for it in a big way and all hell broke loose. Arsenal fans went in all directions; so did almost everyone else, for that matter. I left our lot and grabbed this woman's cases, explaining that I wanted to help her to her train like a good citizen. Really I was doing my best to avoid looking anything like a football fan and, in particular, an Arsenal fan. This woman must have thought I was either trying to nick her stuff or raving mad, but she soon realised that a major fight was about to break out and ran with me to the nearest available platform to escape the melee.

The Scousers were having the time of their lives, and they raided every shop they could get into. It must have been heaven for them – they just took anything and everything they could get their hands on and no one was attempting to stop them. I was buggered if I would either.

Some of the other gits were busy searching for anybody who looked remotely like a football fan, and many innocent people were getting slapped. The whole scene was total chaos.

Then I saw one of the most amazingly stupid things I've ever seen. The Old Bill, who had been well run at the start, sent the horses in. Can you imagine anything so stupid? I mean, horses inside Euston station! They were sliding all over the place. Actually, it was quite hysterical, but it just added to the mayhem. The Scousers were having a field day, and now they turned on the coppers, throwing everything they could at the ones on horseback and fighting those on foot. For about ten minutes, the Scousers owned Euston station. I think they definitely took the chance to pay back the police for a few things that day. The Old Bill were crapping it, and eventually pulled out and left them to it, but after about ten minutes it all calmed down and the Scousers started to make their way down to the trains. They were making so much noise it was deafening, but as soon as it started to subside a bit, the coppers were back in and nicking as many people as they could get their hands on. Of course, these weren't the ringleaders, who were on the trains by now; they were the poor sods who had tried to stay out of the way. Christ knows what happened to them in court. I bet they got well hammered.

I still find it hard to believe that some prat sent the horses into Euston that day. If I hadn't seen it with my own eyes, I'd never have believed it. But the fact that they were there in the first place suggests that the Bill had been expecting something to go off, which makes it even worse because they had time to think about it. I imagine that after what happened someone got a right bollocking, and I don't expect I'll ever see horses inside Euston again.

There is an unwritten rule among London clubs which has, in our experience at least, held true for many years. When you are outside London and you meet another London club, you talk, you play mob football or you join up, but you do not fight. There are obvious exceptions to this, as there are clubs which, with the best will in the world, will never really get on, the prime example being West Ham and Millwall. There have, however, been many examples of truly fantastic inter-supporter football matches at service stations involving up to a hundred players, which have been a more than adequate substitute for a row for those involved. Unfortunately, it should also be noted that there have been many cases of London clubs joining forces to either overrun a service station or combat a rival mob, clubs which, if they were playing each other, would be at it hammer and tongs. In the main, it is of course the smaller clubs that benefit from this rule as they are generally seen as easy targets when travelling. I well remember one occasion when we pulled into a station up north to find some Fulham fans getting a seeing-to from a group of Tranmere supporters who were not clever enough to realise that the impending arrival of seven coachloads of Charlton spelled a great deal of trouble for them – trouble which took about twenty seconds to turn up.

These days, service stations are far safer places to be than they were in the seventies and eighties, something that can be attributed in no small part to the introduction of closed-circuit television in the car parks. The days of jumping back in the transit after a ruck and getting on the motorway and away, are long gone as the police can be after you in minutes and will have the evidence they need to put you away. The hit-and-run tactic is saved for other arenas these days. The next offering is the only exception to the unwritten rule that Londoners don't attack each other we came across, and it is reproduced here only to illustrate the fact that this rule exists, that everyone knows it and that almost everyone abides by it.

The Unwritten Rule

We were on a coach travelling back from a game up north when the driver actually relented and stopped at a service station so that we could all have a quick piss. As the service station was packed solid, a couple of us decided to run across the bridge to the station on the other side, so we steamed over, had a piss and got some stuff from the shop before starting to run back to the side where the coach was parked. As we got to the steps of the bridge, another group of lads were coming down and, spotting that one of them had a Tottenham shirt on, I said, 'Ah, yids!', which is what most fans call Spurs supporters. On hearing this, one of them turned round and shouted, 'What do you mean, yids?' before smacking me hard in the mouth. As I fell back, this lad just came at me and my mate yelled, 'Stop, stop! We're London!'

On hearing this, the other Spurs fans grabbed this guy, pulled him off me, threw him against a wall and attempted to calm him down. 'Shit, I'm sorry lads,' this guy said. 'Are you all right, mate? I'm sorry about 'im, he's pissed out of his mind.' They calmed the situation down and, on finding out that we were from another London club, asked us about our game. We did the same before steaming off to get our coach, which was by now full of pissed-off fans wanting to go home. None of this helped my split lip or my pride, and my mate gave me shit for not keeping my big mouth shut, a lesson I have never forgotten.

Chapter 10

Abroad

Of the very few times I have ever been ashamed to admit to being a football supporter, only one has not involved either England or an English club side playing abroad. Our reputation as the worst group of interlopers since the Waffen SS, a reputation which largely evolved out of the seventies and eighties, was richly deserved, and it is not difficult to see why the English enjoyed it. You only have to look back to Turin in 1980, where England supporters were tear-gassed by the police after they had rioted at the game against Belgium, to understand why people have hated us all for so long. Almost every fan familiar with the global game knows that almost every single football country is saddled with violence at all levels. However, the type of crowd violence abroad can be far worse than anything England has ever seen, and almost certainly will ever see. It is also important to accept the all-too-often overlooked fact that many countries had a problem with violence among fans long before it became fashionable to blame the English for this pattern. However, while the English fan is held up as the archetypal football thug by all and sundry, supporters in this country do not kill referees or shoot their players because they score own goals, nor do they regularly fire-bomb opponents or attempt to blow up trains used by opposing fans. It is also rare for huge flares to be let off within grounds. In other countries all of these things have happened, and yet we are still regarded as the worst there is.

Nevertheless, to discount the English role in the spread of football violence would be to miss an essential point which is relevant not only to the English team, but also to domestic clubs playing abroad. In the seventies and eighties, when the English came to town it meant only one thing: mayhem. The reasons for this are many and varied. They include the availability of cheap overseas travel, which enabled young men to go abroad, sometimes for the first time ever, cheap booze, the English perception of Johnny Foreigner as being inferior to us and the fans' misguided belief that they were defending the honour of their country. The fact that these thugs were looked upon as total scum by every decent football fan (who make up the vast majority) did not deter them in the slightest, and every cup campaign or England match became yet another battleground, which did the game in this country a tragic disservice.

Such was the impact of English hooliganism that European mobs began to look up to the English firms (if that's the right expression) as the leading exponents of football violence and imagined every game in England to be a bloodbath. It is a sad fact that many of the leading mobs in Europe still have English-style nicknames and carry Union Jacks as some form of badge to link themselves with the British. Despite the fact that these days the average English football fan is unlikely to be interested in violence, little has been done to persuade the European mobs that times have changed. Sad to say, when England or English teams go to another country, the locals see it as a chance to prove their own mettle. This reaction has been witnessed time and time again – the reception Manchester United received in Turkey proves the point. Their actions will eventually provoke a reaction, even from those who would not normally get involved in football violence. Sadly, the English authorities prefer to blame the English fans rather than look to see if it is perhaps the opposition fans who are to blame.

As supporters of Chelsea and Arsenal will testify, people travelling these days are not given the chance to explore the country they are visiting. Instead they are herded like cattle from pillar to post and faced with oppressive policing that does nothing but provoke the very reaction we are so keen to avoid. The FA, the body who are supposed to represent the game *for us*, sit on the fence and do nothing but place restrictions on home fans travelling to games or getting tickets, which does not deter the faithful but simply forces them to travel on their own. Their tactic thus backfires, as the mobs are free to roam. Indeed, the FA have a huge case to answer when it comes to the perception of English fans abroad. If you look back to Euro '88 or Italia '90, when England's reputation was at its lowest ebb, the English fans were treated disgracefully at every turn: ticket allocation methods, accommodation plans, everything went wrong that could go wrong, and no one accepted any blame for the failure of what was supposed to be a highly organised operation. Stories of British tourists being deported even though they were not even in Italy for the football were rife, and reports of people having to go back to get their belongings became the norm. This was, of course, yet another example of how the establishment treats the average supporter with disgust: the resultant complaints and trouble among the fans were seen as merely the football hooliganism they had been expecting rather than a valid protest against the conditions against which there was no redress. The FA just put up their hands and said, 'We've done what we can. What else can we do?' Had they admitted: 'Sorry lads, we got it totally wrong,' it would almost certainly have saved the day. The comedian Keith Allen did a video diary for BBC Television during Italia '90, which proved conclusively that England's fans were treated like dirt by almost everybody, the England manager included. Watching this film, it is easy to understand the fans' frustration. I have to admit here that I have not seen an England game live since 1988. During those championships, we attended all of England's games. The defeat by Holland and the loss to Ireland were bad enough, but the game against Russia, when the team were already out of the competition and, it seemed, could not have cared less about the match, was just too much to bear. The players apparently did not give a jot about the thousands of supporters who had endured having everything thrown at them by other fans, the FA representatives and the media, but who had continued to support the team regardless. It was a pathetic display to watch, with no sign of pride or honour, and the side let down the country and us in the biggest possible way because they did not even seem to try. I swore on the way home from that game that I would never watch another England game until that attitude changed, and things have yet to improve enough for me even to consider it.

Of course, the period we are talking about here was bereft of any club involvement from England because of one terrible disaster: Heysel. The circumstances behind the organisation of that game are a staggering indictment of UEFA, because it is hard to imagine anybody getting anything so disastrously wrong. A dilapidated stadium holding a major European Cup final, terrible policing with little or no planning and two sets of highly volatile fans were a recipe for tragedy. Maybe someone convinced the Belgians or UEFA that because it was Liverpool playing and not, for example, Tottenham or Arsenal, there would be lots of singing rather than any trouble; the well-known Scouse propensity for good-natured banter and getting along with everyone would surely make this a Cup final to remember, even though the Juventus fans were well known for their vicious streak. Well, sadly, if that was the case, they got it horribly wrong. The game will of course never be forgotten, not because of the humour and the singing, but because some Liverpool fans caused the death of almost forty people before a ball had been kicked. On the night of this despicable act, I was still in the Royal Air Force and working in northern Germany with a squadron of Phantom aircraft whose staff were almost entirely Scottish. Also on the base at the time was a squadron of aircraft from Belgium. I watched the events unfold as the only Englishman in a room full of Belgians on a TV with German commentary. I have never forgotten how the people I had been working with for two happy weeks now looked at me with utter disgust because, to them, I represented a nationality which had caused the death of almost forty people in their country. I slunk away ashamed of my own country for the only time in my life. None of them spoke to me or any other Englishman for the remainder of their stay, because of the horrendous behaviour of those Liverpool fans.

The fact that some Liverpool fans tried to shift the blame for that dreadful event on to other people was almost as disgraceful as the riot itself. It was claimed that there were Chelsea fans in the crowd and that National Front agitators had started the trouble. But there was no evidence for any of this. Even the subsequent conviction of fourteen supporters for their part in the trouble was accompanied by a pitiful series of press interviews with whining fans pleading innocence to avoid deportation, most of which were later shown to be untrue. The fact that all clubs were subsequently banned from Europe was inevitable: we all had to suffer for what they did, and clubs like Wimbledon, whose fans missed out on the glory of European football, suffered more than most. The removal of the ban and the subsequent pathetic reduction of the ban on Liverpool, even post-Hillsborough, were scant reward for the wilderness years, especially when you look at the problems encountered in other European countries such as Italy, Holland, Germany and Turkey, none of whom has ever received anything worse than a slap on the wrists from UEFA for the behaviour of their supporters.

In 1995 there was an apparent upsurge in the trouble involving English fans abroad – although, as we all know, it never really went away in the first place. However, this time there was one notable difference: much of the violence was inflicted *on* fans by some obscene policing methods which seemed to involve beating the shit out of anyone who looked English, no matter what the reason or provocation, if any existed at all. The trouble involving Chelsea fans in Belgium and Spain was so ludicrous that it became the source of great humour afterwards: some of the things that happened were so far-fetched that they were laughable. A report of a bloke sitting on the toilet with the dreaded 'trots' who had the gross misfortune to be attacked by a copper with a big stick certainly gave us a chuckle or two. But the disturbing side to these incidents, which has not been properly looked at by either the media or the FA, is the way that the British government allowed its citizens to be badly treated without any condemnation whatsoever. If a few coachloads of athletics fans, or rugby supporters for that matter, travelled abroad to watch their team play and were attacked by the police with little or no provocation, the government of the day, the press and the public would be outraged, and quite rightly so. Yet when football supporters are involved no one in authority says anything. The perception that these supporters 'got what they deserved' is offensive at the very least. The vast majority of fans in this country are decent, law-abiding, taxpaying voters who watch football for enjoyment. Football supporters neither deserve nor expect to be treated badly for following it and if we are, whether at home or abroad, we expect – no, demand – that the authorities intervene on our behalf. When they do not, we have every right to kick up as much stink as we possibly can. Of course, there are bound to be times when people do indeed get what they deserve, and we have absolutely no sympathy for anybody who travels to matches with the express purpose of causing trouble, because these people are indeed among the worst elements within our game and do nothing but bring shame on the rest of us. If they do this abroad, the countries concerned should not deport them back here, where they will escape punishment, but should take them to court and deal with them exactly as they would their own citizens. These individuals know that they will get off scot-free – that's why they do it. A few years in a foreign nick is the best deterrent we can imagine.

It would be impossible to discuss England without looking in depth at what happened in Dublin on 15 February 1995, because was without doubt one of the worst nights of orchestrated football violence there has ever been. Even now, months later, we still find it difficult to believe, not only what happened on that night, but that people involved in the game as a whole could be so stupid as to let it happen and then be surprised that it did. If ever there was a game that was sure to provoke a major incident, it was this one, as has been confirmed by the report of the BNP member given in Chapter 5. The political situation at the time, coupled with the extreme right-wing politics and known Loyalist links of a small but significant number of travelling England fans, made it almost certain. It is well known by both the police and the FA that certain clubs have supporters with strong political beliefs, particularly regarding Ireland, and they had a duty to deal with the problem before it occurred. It seems they did not. The police in England had already acknowledged this fact and had spent huge amounts of time (so they would have you believe) finding out who was travelling when, how and why. This information was then passed to the Irish police and football authorities, who apparently did nothing but weigh into supporters when it eventually went off. If they had expended as much energy at air and ferry ports and on dealing with the various ticket touts outside the ground, the problems might never have arisen or been much reduced.

Of course, the press went to town. Some of the rubbish that was written was quite astonishing, but the most amazing thing was that most people were surprised that violence at football was planned. Where have they been all this time? Has the game never been aware of the firms, mobs and crews that exist within the game? Of course they have, but by dragging up all the old stuff again, it was easy to pretend that it was all new, in spite of the fact that anyone who watches the game can tell you that it's all as old as the hills. The condemnation of English fans which followed this game was swift and deserved, but many of the questions which arose in the aftermath have remained unanswered. One of the most sinister is this: if the police and the government knew exactly who was travelling and where from, why did they not take action to restrict their movements? Was it that these fans were allowed to travel in the hope that they would indeed cause trouble to disrupt a fledgling Northern Ireland peace process? The account we were given suggests that this may have been what happened. This would raise the question of who in authority would want to do this. If that is not the explanation, then the only alternative we can come up with is sheer incompetence.

However, despite these events, all is not doom and gloom and things are getting back to how they should be. England will host the European Championships in 1996 while the post-Taylor (both Graham and Lord Justice) years have given the game in this country a new optimism. We now have the stadiums to grace any match and teams which are showing how good the game is when played in the British way, that great blood-and-guts style that can beat anyone. The fact that these championships are taking place in England shows that even the powers that be recognise that the demise of violence within grounds is continuing apace. At the time of writing, we can only hope that the Italian, German and Dutch fans, who will obviously come to watch their teams, do not try to bring it back. That must not be allowed to happen; if it does it could set everything back years. We have come too far for that.

A word of caution, though: we do not imagine for one second that anyone will be able to control what happens outside in the pubs and the clubs. There are scores to be settled and there are too many people wanting to settle them. It is well known among fans that extreme political bodies such as Combat 18 are recruiting at certain clubs with a view to causing disruption at Euro '96 in support of the national side, but what is not so well known is that the Anti-Nazi League have also been recruiting fans with the aim of attacking any supporters' group with right-wing elements – in short, almost every group in Europe. It will be interesting to see what measures both the FA and the police will put in place to deal with the threat of violence away from the grounds during Euro '96, but it will be just as interesting to see what their reaction is if it all goes wrong and violence does erupt, especially if it doesn't involve England fans, but Germans or Italians. Just who will the FA blame then?

PART FIVE
The Victims of Violence

Chapter 11   *Victims*

Chapter 12   *Hillsborough*

Chapter 11
Victims

In any violent incident, as in any form of contest, there will inevitably be a loser, the person who comes off worse and leaves the scene with a black eye or a bloody nose. In a mass brawl it therefore follows that there can be plenty of victims, as has been seen on many, many occasions, and some of the injuries can be terrible; indeed, even fatal. However, as with most kinds of violence, the real victims are the innocent bystanders, the people who suffer intimidation, aggression and abuse and, worst of all, fear. In the context of football violence there are many thousands of victims, from the people who simply will not go to games in case they become involved in anything to the supporters who, week in, and week out, suffer the legacy of the early seventies in the shape of such indignities as segregation and high-profile policing. The local population, too, suffers, through disruption to their daily lives, which reflects on the game and, indirectly, on us. These are the real victims of crowd trouble, because the actions of other people have had, and continue to have, a direct effect on what they want to do. Football in general suffers, as a result of a crap image. It has also suffered in the past from diminishing crowds, but one positive factor is that over the last few seasons attendances have been rising.

As we all know, football grounds these days are great places to visit and the public are, in general, perfectly safe. Yes, of course the atmosphere might be hostile and the language colourful, to say the least, but that's what supporting football is all about for the vast majority of spectators. That's why we all go – men, women and children. But the overriding consideration has to be that you will be safe. Even outside the ground, if you act naturally and go about your business in a normal manner without doing things that might provoke others, you will almost certainly not be molested by anyone else. Now, we do not wish to give the impression that the problem of crowd violence has disappeared – it most certainly has not – but it is obvious to anyone who spectates on a regular basis that the vast majority of games played in England are incident-free. Much of the credit for that has to go to the supporters, who were sick and tired of walking along with one eye over their shoulder all the time. It is better now, more friendly and enjoyable with, at most places, an atmosphere to match. So why is football not publicising the fact? Why, at Watford, for example, do we see the odd appallingly constructed advert in one of the local papers, but nothing in the rest? Why can a club afford to pay a player thousands of pounds a week but not spend any money on television advertising? We don't know the answer to that, but it is obvious to us that advertising is the best way to draw in new punters, and if done properly it would enhance the image of the sport among the non-supporting public and make them aware that football is not the thugs' playground many people would have them believe it is. Those thugs who do go are really only interested in taking on like-minded people, not families on a day out.

While we have, we hope, established that the greatest victim of crowd trouble has been the 'average' supporter, it cannot be denied that over the years a lot of people have felt a more immediate and physical effect. Many have been seriously hurt as a result of this violence. Sadly, we have seen people take some serious beatings at games just as we have seen others inflicting them, but even worse than that is the fact that not all of them were involved with football at all. It is one thing to go to a game in a mob and end up taking a hiding, but what must it be like to be going about your business and suddenly faced with a horde of yobs intent on beating the shit out of you? Fine if you've been there before, and if you know the game you'll know roughly what to do and expect, but what if you had nothing at all to do with football? What if the nearest thing to any form of violence you have ever experienced has been watching it on television? Imagine if it was your mum or your granddad. Can you comprehend the absolute terror that must overwhelm people who find themselves in that position? If you can even begin to imagine that, you can start to understand why people do not like football supporters.

It is one thing to be attacked and beaten up in the name of football, but it is quite another for that attack to involve the use of any form of weapon – that is cowardice of the very worst kind. We're not talking about the type of row involving the throwing of bricks or bottles, but about the carrying of items designed to inflict terrible damage and/or pain or another individual, something we struggle to comprehend. Over the years, certain groups have become known for their love of a specific weapon. For example, you knew full well that if you were playing a team from Liverpool, then some supporters would almost certainly be armed with Stanley blades to slice through clothes and skin. You knew that if a mob was travelling on a special, the metal strips in the bottom of the window blinds would be removed for throwing at you just as you quickly learned that a newspaper folded in a particular way could be transformed into the dreaded 'Millwall brick', as solid, and as capable of inflicting as much pain, as any rock, if used correctly. These days the inventive minds among the mobs have devised some horrific weaponry for use at football, such as the use of two Stanley blades taped together with a matchstick in between. (The resultant cut is almost impossible to stitch and leaves a horrific scar.) Moreover, increased access to Europe and America has seen the spread of concealed weapons, readily available over the counter, such as a trouser belt containing a 12-inch blade and rings which can easily be turned into knuckledusters and anti-rape substances like Mace, which will render anyone helpless in seconds.

We have all seen coins and darts being thrown inside grounds (thankfully, not very often these days) but we have also been told of many other kinds of missile attacks: petrol-bomb blitzes by Newcastle fans, golf balls with pieces of razor blade stuck in them (Cardiff) and even a sniper targeting some Man City fans waiting for a train – a Barnsley supporter with an airgun. However, there is one weapon above all others that is gaining a reputation with the mobs, and that is CS gas. As an ex-serviceman, Dougie was exposed to CS gas quite regularly during chemical warfare training, it is bloody unpleasant stuff. Like Mace, it is classed as an incapacitant, which means that it renders the person on the receiving end incapable of doing anything other than coughing their guts up. Your eyes sting like mad, your nose runs and your skin burns like it does the day after you've had a bad dose of the sun. If you wash with warm water within twelve hours, the heat will cause the particles in the gas to start working again and it will be just as bad as the first time. The use of this gas is simple and effective: fire up the canister, throw it through a pub window and either do a runner or wait for the opposition, who will be coughing, spluttering and probably terrified, to come to you, where you do the obvious.

We know that this gas has already been used in attacks by groups from Middlesbrough, Swansea, Portsmouth and Shrewsbury, and I am sure that there have been, and will be, others because, despite being illegal in Britain, these canisters are, for some inexplicable reason, readily available in Europe. The worst thing about CS from a mob point of view is that there are only two real defences: a decent gas respirator and approximately 50 yards distance (upwind, of course). So if you get hit with it, you're immediately finished. The police have got to get on top of this one somehow, which is easy to say – it will prove almost impossible for them to do.

There are, of course, other weapons in general use among the mobs – cigarette packets and drink cans full of stones or cement (easily concealed), socks of pool balls, and so on – and it would be easy to provide a list pages long. In short, anyone involved in any form of trouble would use anything they could lay their hands on if the situation demanded it. There is no cure for the use of weapons other than for the supporters themselves to build on the unwritten rules already in place – a sort of code of practice, if you like – and declare it what we southerners would call 'bang out of order' to use or carry any weapon. We will not hold our breath.

There follow some accounts from people who have themselves been on the receiving end of violence from football supporters, and they make tragic reading in that they are only the very tip of the iceberg. While the actual content of these reports varies, there can be no doubt that the final message is the same, and it is a very simple one: please stop it, and stop it soon.

Swansea Away

It was in the mid-eighties, 1983, I think, and we had travelled to Swansea down the dreaded M4 – four of us in my car, which was the normal thing in those days. The others just messed around and caused havoc at the service stations while I kept a reasonably cool head and got us away quickly if anything happened. Although we knew that Swansea had a reputation, we certainly weren't worried. We hadn't yet been run by anybody that season, in spite of trouble with some big names. This was our first season in the First Division, the big time, and both the team and us were doing the business.

Our arrival at the ground was the usual thing. We parked outside the prison, which was a giggle, and the usual taunts aimed at the locals were far more vocal than normal because these weren't just a different team, they were foreign. The ground itself was exactly what we had expected – crap – but we cheered up considerably when word spread among our lads that there was a mob of Welshmen up the back. They were obviously in with us to suss things out, but as far as we were concerned they were our sport. It didn't take long for it all to go off, although they were tossers, just loads of mouth and hoping that the police would get them out quick before they got hurt. No such luck. A few mighty blows were delivered before the Bill got in and they were rescued.

The slapping we dealt out put us in a hearty mood, though, and what with the team winning again, we were in great spirits leaving the ground, which is when it all started to go wrong. On our way back to the car park, this same mob of Swansea came down the road towards us. We just kept on and walked right through them, and the expected row never occurred, just the normal shouts of 'Cockney wankers' and other original abuse.

We were at the jail, ready to cross the road to the car park, when we heard the running and the shouts coming from behind us. We were caught, and we were in trouble. The four of us split and ran across the main road and through the car park, but, being older, slower and probably plain stupid, I stopped near my car while the others vanished. I turned and they were on me, surrounding me before I knew it, about ten of them and me on my own. I looked around and could see that all the cars around me contained my so-called 'colleagues', but they were all the dreaded mums and dads, and the sound of the door-lock buttons going down was almost deafening. 'Bollocks,' I thought. 'This is it.'

I searched around for the leader – there's always a leader, and this time he stood out a mile because of the bloody great lump of wood he had in his hand. 'Well, Cockney, where do you want this?'

Straight away, his voice and his tone pissed me off, but good sense prevailed. 'Look, mate, I don't want any trouble.'

'Too bad, it's here,' he said, and I quickly looked around to see that not only were his mates ready for it, but I now had carloads of our fans hoping that they would see some-one get a good kicking just to round off their day.

My mind was racing, but there was only one thing I could do. If I was going to get a kicking, this bastard in front of me was going to catch at least one, and the biggest one, I could get in. 'Come on, then, cunt,' I screamed. 'Let's fucking go!' I started to run forward, aware that his mates had stepped back, stunned, and that he was just standing there looking at me. I had caught them on the hop, and it suddenly occurred to me that I might be able to slap him one and get past before they knew what was happening. That would at least give me a chance. However, before I could move any further, he realised what was going on and smashed the wood across the side of my knee. I dropped like a stone, curling into a ball before I hit the ground so that the expected kicking would do as little damage as possible.

As I lay there, someone screamed, 'Leave him, get the other bastard!' and they vanished. I couldn't believe it. I just lay there for a couple of seconds and then sat up. They had gone. Thank Christ for that. Now I vented my anger on all the cars parked around me, because, as I saw it, they had let me down, and that meant they had let the club down. 'You fucking cowards!' I screamed.

I made it over to my car and just leaned against it. My leg was killing me, but I felt a mixture of relief, anger and shame, because although I had got away with it, someone had beaten me, and that had never happened at a game before. Suddenly, I heard some noise from somewhere. They were back. Once they saw me I became their target again and was quickly surrounded. This time it was worse because it wasn't just me, they might total my car as well and the fact that they were holding various lumps of brick just confirmed my fears. 'Well, well, look who's 'ere.' The leader stepped forward again.

'OK, mate, fair enough.' I tried to sound convincing, but I was bloody terrified. 'Please, mate, not the car.'

He stood there looking at me, and the blokes with him started to shout. It was coming again at any moment, or so I thought. Then the leader said, 'Leave 'im, he's had enough,' in that horrible bloody accent.

'Thanks, mate,' I said. 'Thanks a lot.'

He looked at me again and said, 'Look, I'm not your fuckin' mate, right?' and then they turned and ran off, hurling abuse at everyone nearby.

I was suddenly exhausted. I climbed into my car to wait for the others. When they returned, it became clear that two had escaped but the other one, who had stopped to see where I was, had got a real hiding. We later found out he had a fractured skull. It must have been him they had gone after when they left me.

The following week, our game was on the Sunday. But Swansea were at Spurs on the Saturday, and that was where we would be. This time we would be really ready and do those bastards for what they had done to us. Word of our beating had spread, and so we had no difficulty in getting a decent mob together, and while normally we would be seriously apprehensive at the thought of taking a group to White Hart Lane and going into the Spurs end, this time we were after revenge. Spurs held no interest for us – it was Welshmen we wanted.

There was no way in the world that we could hide about twenty blokes standing on the old Shelf, so we soon became the target for huge amounts of abuse from the Spurs fans. But as we were giving out loads of noise ourselves, they saw us as something of a novelty, I think. It looked as if Swansea had a few down and so we left the game early and went to the back of the away end to find the gates open and nobody about. We steamed up the stairs screaming blue murder, only to see a collection of mums, dads and kids. Just crap away support and the wankers we were after absent – there wasn't even anything like a mob with them.

We were well gutted and felt cheated. We had put ourselves out for this lot and had risked a hiding from Spurs at the same time. That hiding taught me a few things, though, the most important being that I'll never run again. It's better to stand and fight, even to take a few, but don't run.

While the previous account was from someone who had been involved in football violence, the one that follows illustrates the effect a violent mob can have on people unconnected with football. It also shows how sometimes things can go so far that even those involved are surprised and alarmed. However the circumstances of the incident also prove just why it will always be impossible to get rid of football-related violence, even if the game and the grounds are safe.

The Fatman

Loads of us had been to Chelsea that day to see the Blues do the business over Sheffield Wednesday. They were the usual crap northern team and we'd given them loads of grief during the game, as you do – no rows or anything: the law have got all that sussed inside the grounds now. But they had quite a big mob down and some of them had tried it on in a few pubs before the game, nothing serious. After the match we gave them the usual run down on the tube. These fuckin' northerners can't get to grips with the tube trains.

Anyway, they were shit, and we saw them all off pretty quickly. So our lot decided to go up the King's Road for the night and pick up a Sloaney or two if we could. So we settled into this bar and got into a nice Saturday-night session when this other little mob of about ten or so Chelsea came in. I knew a few of them and recognised the rest, so we had a bit of a chat about what had gone off that day, and after about half an hour went back into our own groups.

Later on, this row started to develop over by the bar. One of the Chelsea boys was giving this barmaid some verbal so they wanted him out. The bouncers were coming over to get him and all his mates started to front them up.

We stayed out of it because you just don't do that sort of thing in a bar, especially one of your favourites, and as far as we were concerned, this was their problem – it was nothing to do with football, or us, for that matter. The bouncers were all there by this time and they started to wade in to sort out the Chelsea lads. But the one who had caused all the bother was arguing with one of the barmen. All of a sudden, he picked up a glass and stuffed it straight into the barman's face.

This poor fucker's face just exploded, and everything sort of went into slow motion like it does in an accident or something. Before anyone could react, this bastard just screamed, *'Go, go!'* and they all legged it with a load of the bouncers steaming after them. The barman was screaming his fucking head off and that started the barmaids off and then all these tarts in the bar started going mental. It was bloody mayhem in there. Well, I'm a qualified first-aider – I have to be in my job – and so I dived over the bar to help this guy, because he was in big trouble. His face was sort of peeled open where this cunt had put the glass in and twisted it. He was going into shock, which was calming him down a little, and I got some ice on to his face to try to keep the swelling down until an ambulance got there.

Suddenly, one of the bouncers screamed: 'He's one of the bastards!' and pointed straight at me.

'Fuck off, mate, I'm trying to help him here,' was all I could say before this bloke lumps me one on the side of the head. At that, all my mates went for it and we literally fought our way out of that place before the law got there. Everybody went for us as if it was us who had started all the trouble: Christ, we were just sat there minding our own business. We got out, but not before a lot more people had been hurt, and we fucked off rapid because by that time the sirens were approaching and there was no way we were getting tugged. I had been trying to *help* this bloke.

So we dived on to this passing bus and were away. We couldn't use the tube station opposite the bar because of the closed-circuit television – the Filth would have got our pictures. From there, we went up West and into another bar, where we tried to take in what had happened and how we had got roped in. On reflection it was obvious: we had been talking to this mob earlier and two plus two equals five in the average bouncer's book. After about an hour, who should turn up at this bar but this fucking mob. Within about two seconds we were over and dragging them outside. They were going to get a slapping because of the way they had put us in the frame for their ruck. As we got them out, they were shouting and screaming at us and it became clear that the bastards were scared shitless – but not of us. I calmed one of them down a bit and he gave me the full story about what had happened in the bar and afterwards.

He told me that there was one bloke with them who was trouble wherever they went and always got them involved. There was no way they could get rid of him as he lived near them and went to every game, home and away, just like they did. Earlier in the day he had got a slapping off some Wednesday fans on the tube. In the bar, he'd been well pissed and, they thought, doped up on something, and he was after revenge. This barman giving him verbal just sent him off on one and so he just glassed him and started lashing out at everything that moved, including some of his own group when they had escaped. When they got outside, they did the same thing as we had: dived on a bus and went upstairs. While they were up there, they started shouting and all that bollocks to let off steam because they were so hyped. I mean, how would you feel after being involved in something like that?

The only other people on the bus with them were this bloke and his bird, and these lads soon started to get a bit mouthy about women in general, you know the sort of thing. Suddenly, our boy called over to this bloke and asked him if his bird was a good fuck. The poor cow was so embarrassed because they were all laughing at her and this bloke did not know what to do. They stood up and moved towards the stairs to get away, but our boy was having none of that. He told them to sit down or there would be trouble. Apparently, he then insisted on this bloke answering his question. The poor bastard tried to ignore everything that was going on.

Then our boy dropped a bombshell. He told this lad he was going to rape his bird. Well, as you can imagine, she went mad and he stood up and called this bloke an animal or something and that was it. Our man is across the seats like Colin Jackson on acid and wallops this geezer right in the face, dives down on top of him and they start rolling around between the seats. Suddenly, he gets up and shouts out: 'Look what I've got 'ere!' and he's got this bloke's fucking ear in his mouth. He had bitten his ear right off! Not surprisingly, this bloke is screaming his fucking head off and so is his bird. Then the conductor appeared and he started as well.

That was it. The rest of this little crew did the off leaving this mad cunt on the bus and got as far away as they could, eventually ending up where they had met us again.

In view of all this, I decided that we were in serious trouble. The Filth would be all over the place looking for us and would certainly be at the Bridge for the next home game. As I had been seen with the barman, I would be a prime candidate – they would have a wonderful description of me. In a situation like this, there are only two things you can do, and we had to decide which one pretty quickly because there were about twenty blokes in the frame for what this arsehole had done. I know that a lot of people are going to be disgusted at this, but the first thing we thought about was shopping this wanker to the law. Yes, I do know that no one likes a grass, but fuck me, this was serious. Anyway, a few of the lads were dead against it so the only other option was to stay away from the Bridge for a while until it all cooled off which, as it happened, is exactly what we did.

In fact the bloke in question was nicked later that night.

After getting off the bus, he had got involved in something else and the law got him. He was eventually put inside for a while. Thank fuck for that.

This story, from Dave C. of Maidenhead, shows how the smallest thing can provoke an attack – sometimes from the unlikeliest sources. If he had not known how to handle himself, then the results could have been much worse. It is this sort of almost indiscriminate violence that again shows how big the problem is.

Nottingham

Let me start this by telling you a few background facts about me which are important to this story. First, I am Scottish; secondly I support Falkirk, and thirdly, I wouldn't go to watch an English team if I was paid. This story is purely a result of being in the wrong place at the wrong time but is absolutely true.

A few years ago, my two business partners and I decided to spend Christmas in Nottingham for a variety of reasons, not least of which was that the place is overrun with women. After a great Friday night out, we had just finished the Saturday dinnertime session and were on our way back to our hotel for a sleep and a shower before another night out. While I knew there was a game on, I hadn't given it a second thought. As we walked towards the city centre, we stopped to look in an estate agent's window and were laughing at the prices of the houses compared to those where we live, as you do, when this small group of blokes came along. All of a sudden, one of them stopped and said to me: 'Are you laughing at our town?'

The seriousness of this situation did not register with me at all. I just turned, stared at him and started laughing because it was such a totally stupid question. However, when he insisted: 'Are you Birmingham fans laughing at our town?' and I saw my two so-called friends legging it up the road, I began to sober up rapidly and realised I was in big trouble. Before I could move, they all piled into me. My only thought was to stay on my feet and try to get away, which I managed to do despite the fact that I had taken a few good whacks.

As I pushed clear and ran up the road after my mates, I realised that my shirt was covered in blood and a quick check showed that my nose was pouring. I had obviously taken a good thump, but there was no way I could slow down as this mob were after me. They were getting closer all the time and I thought that the best thing I could do was to try to get the police. On the other side of the road was this boy of about fifty or so who was watching what was happening and appeared quite concerned, so I ran across the road to ask for help. As I got close to him, he pulled his leg back and kicked me straight in the balls, shouting: 'You Brummie bastard!'

I couldn't believe what was happening. All the lot from up the road let out a big cheer and ran towards me even faster, and now this old boy was up for it as well, so all I could do was get up and run (or rather, stagger) into town. As I rounded the next corner, I spotted the blokes I was with. They were in that 'scared but pissing themselves laughing' sort of mood, which did not go down too well with me. But at least they had rung the police, who had told them that they were on their way and to stay in the city square where we would be easily spotted and fairly safe. After five anxious minutes, we saw this police car and waved it down, but did it stop? Did it, bollocks, but at least the mob after me did a runner. On its third circuit of the square, the police car pulled over and I went mental at them because they hadn't stopped. The copper thought we were waving to him to wish him a 'Happy Christmas!'. To add insult to injury, he added that all he could do was give us a lift back to the hotel, because even if he did manage to arrest anyone, they would all stick up for each other, and that besides, I hadn't come off too badly considering how many of them there were. As you can imagine, I was stunned, but there was nothing I could do.

Looking back on it now, even I can see the funny side of it, but I really hope with all my heart that the old boy who kicked me in the balls becomes incontinent very, very soon.

The following incident, which was widely reported in the local press, is even more alarming, because it reveals that violent supporters can be attracted to even the smallest games. Despite the precautions taken by the school in question, trouble still broke out. There is possibly no clearer example in this book of how football is used as an excuse for violence.

Denefield School

I have just returned from one of the most disgusting, terrifying and upsetting experiences of my life, let alone my time following football. What do you think the occasion was? West Ham–Millwall? The Old Firm derby, perhaps? Maybe even Leeds–Man United? No, it was none of these. It was an English Schools FA Under-16 Trophy semi-final between Denefield School near Reading and my own son's school, St Michael's of Garston, played at Reading Town (yes, Town) FC on Tuesday 9 May 1995. What should have been the greatest sporting achievement for the school and one of the proudest moments for all the boys, the parents and the teachers will be remembered as one of the worst moments we have ever experienced.

This was actually a semi-final replay. The first game had been seen as a missed opportunity because we had led 2–0 with ten minutes to go, threw it away and ended up drawing 2–2. The crowd of about 500 included a good number from Reading, and we had all seen a great little game in a nice trouble-free atmosphere – just what you would expect of a schoolboy game. As you can imagine, everyone was excited about the second leg, but as we arrived at the small stadium for the match, I noticed how untidy both the surrounding area and the ground were. I also noticed that a lot of the supporters from Denefield School who had been at our place were not here for the home game, but something was there that I had never seen at a schoolboy fixture before: there were two policemen present.

The first half of the game itself went really well and our 250 supporters saw the boys win the game in the first half as they went in 3–0 up at the break. During this period, I had begun to notice a group of locals who had gathered together and were walking round the pitch abusing some of our pupils in the crowd. They then began to hurl insults at the players and things started to get a bit nasty, so one of the parents went over and asked them to be quiet and calm down. The torrent of abuse and aggression they received from this group was disgusting, and so we went over to the policemen and asked them to do something about it which, to be fair, they did, and a few of these louts cleared off.

Once the game was over and the boys had finished celebrating their victory with the supporters, we waited for them to shower and change before leaving. The PE teacher from Denefield congratulated us on the win and apologised for the trouble caused by what he believed were ex-pupils just hanging about. He also took the trouble to explain that he had not been at all happy about the staging of the game at this ground because it was in an area of the town which had a bad reputation. It was he who had requested the presence of the police – a good thing, as it turned out.

As we started to board the coaches for the journey home, we noticed that the locals had returned, but this time in greater numbers. As our boys came out of the changing room, the local lads surrounded their coach and started to abuse them and push them around. A few of the parents quickly moved in to sort this out. Suddenly, one of the dads fell back holding his face. He had been cut across the nose with what all of us initially thought was a razor blade but what was in fact his own glasses being broken as he was punched. Can you believe that, at a game like this! There was blood everywhere, but luckily the cut was not that deep and so we decided to get on the coaches and get out of there as quickly as we could.

The locals appeared to have turned and run at the sight of the blood, but as we finally all got on our coach there were two loud bangs. One of the side windows came right through and the windscreen was cracked. This was unbelievable. We were all in total shock and could not understand what on earth was happening. More police arrived and started to escort us away from the ground towards the motorway, but as we left more rocks came at the coaches from all angles. The police seemed powerless to stop it and just got us away as fast as they could.

All the way home we sat in silence, totally shellshocked at what had taken place. Even as I write this I still find it hard to believe it really happened. You hear about this sort of thing at League games – although I've never actually seen anything like it at any match myself – but I would never, ever have believed that anything like this would occur at schoolboy football. Is this what it's come to now?

The sort of incident related below, by Barry of Slough, shows again how difficult it used to be to escape violence on the terraces. Fortunately, this sort of situation is much rarer now than it was then, but the effects on him were long-lasting.

Chelsea

This happened years ago – it must have been the early seventies because I was still at school and Chelsea's second colours were red, green and white then. Every home game, I went to watch Chelsea. I don't think I had missed a match that season but this one was to be my last. I can't even remember who else was playing, but it must have been a Cup game because I'm sure that Arsenal were playing Millwall that week, which could only happen in the Cup, even these days. My mate and I stood on the Shed, which at that time was probably the most dangerous terrace in the country. We usually stood at the side because the fights – there was always a fight – used to happen in the middle behind the goal. Such was the reputation of Chelsea at that time that most fights were between rival gangs of Blue fans, because no one else ever came near the Shed then.

However, for some reason at this particular game we were standing near the middle, and early on in the match it happened right in front of us. This gap just opened up and there was this group rucking in a big way, and they meant business. We just stood back and watched it all – it was the first fight we had ever really seen close up. It wasn't that we hadn't seen violence before – in those days the terraces and the tube stations were a battleground most Saturdays – it was just that this fight was there, right in front of us.

Suddenly, someone pulled out a blade. Everyone just pushed away from this guy as he waved this knife around like mad. My mate and I tried to duck under everyone else to get out, right out. Clive, my mate, suddenly flew back, he must have been hit or pushed, and he was standing right in front of this guy, who by then was ready to stick anybody. Before I knew what was happening, I had flown round and kicked this bloke just under his right arm, and he went flying. I don't know why I did it; it must have just been an instinctive reaction. I grabbed Clive and we ran, because by this time the law were pouring in and the dogs usually came early at Chelsea in those days. We steamed out of the ground. Clive was crying, I think, and I was absolutely terrified that either this bloke would be after me or I would get nicked. We just headed for home as quickly as we could, two scared teenagers who had thought that they were untouchable. To this day, I've never been back.

The attacking of an obvious innocent is something we regard as the worst form of cowardice, and any attempt to justify it merely makes the original act even more pathetic. I wonder if the so-called hard-man in the account which follows would fancy kicking someone wearing a West Ham or Chelsea shirt outside Upton Park or Stamford Bridge. Somehow, I doubt it.

Sheffield United

I'm a student living in Sheffield and, as I am a Bristol City fan, I went to watch my team play the Blades intent on enjoying myself whatever the score. Despite the 3–0 stuffing, we left the away end in good spirits, taking the mickey out of how poor our team were. I went with four other people, two males and two females, all aged about nineteen. I know, looking back, we were naïve, but two of us were wearing City shirts under our jackets while a third, Dave, had his on and his jacket tied round his waist. We began walking along Bramall Lane towards St Mary's Gate roundabout, and were about 50 yards from the ground when some bloke began shouting from across the road in our direction.

We didn't think much of it as there were about a hundred people leaving the ground with us, but the next thing we knew, this bloke had run across the road and had my mate Dave in a headlock as they walked along. He said something along the lines of, 'You're in Sheffield now, and I don't want to see that fucking kit, so cover it up!'

Dave said: 'OK, OK. I don't want any trouble. I'll put my jacket on,' and started to do so.

About 100 yards further on, this bloke stopped us again and said: 'Get that fucking kit off. There's three of us in front and three behind, and if you don't take it off we'll kick your fucking heads in.'

There were still about a hundred people around us at the time and a police van with policemen inside about 5 metres away. As Dave pulled the shirt over his head, this guy kicked him in the shin and another smacked him on the back of the head. Dave fell to the floor and this bloke then said, 'Go under the subway and you're dead!' Dave had a cut under his eye which quickly closed up and also chipped three teeth.

I guess this was only a minor skirmish compared to some, but it was the only incident we have ever been involved in and to us it was horrific. We honestly thought that these yobs had all but disappeared from football, but how wrong we were. We did nothing to incite or invite any trouble; this thug just went for us for no other reason than the fact that we were there and we were City fans.

Chapter 12

Hillsborough

It will come as no surprise that we have received many letters regarding the tragedy at Hillsborough, which was without doubt the catalyst that brought about the dramatic changes in the way we are now forced to watch the game. Some letters were from supporters of Liverpool and some from Forest fans who were there on what was one of British football's blackest days. We even had a letter from a policeman on duty there. We also received many opinions from supporters all over the country on what actually happened. Much has been written regarding the events of that terrible day in 1989, but the following letter seems to echo the thoughts of many of the fans who contacted us. We do not doubt that what is said in this account will prove controversial, but the events at Hillsborough are impossible to ignore. What is beyond doubt is that the poor souls who died that day were the victims of only one thing – football – and they should be in the thoughts of every spectator every Saturday afternoon. That every one of them is watching the great game in a far better place and that their tragic loss changed British football forever are inescapable facts. We can only hope that, in some ridiculous way, their suffering will bring some sort of reasoning for what happened. There but for the grace of God go us all.

A Forest View

Standing in the Kop at Hillsborough that day still seems like a distant and bad memory. I still think to myself, 'Did it really happen? Was I actually there?' and it's strange that the television pictures actually seem more real to me than the images I saw, if that makes any sense. Although I was at Hillsborough, and I have the programme and ticket stub to prove it, I don't for one minute pretend that I can understand the agony and immense loss that those Liverpool supporters and the families of those who died must have felt, and I'm sure will continue to feel for the rest of their lives.

Since that day, the inquiry has gone on and on and probably will be talked about forever. Fingers have been pointed at the police and calls for disciplinary action against individual officers have been long and loud. The FA have also come in for their share of criticism for the allocation of the Leppings Lane end to Liverpool fans when the larger Kop end was obviously more suitable. But is it any surprise that the FA got it wrong? It's not exactly an unusual event, is it?

Being an FA Cup semi-final, the match was of course all-ticket and, as always, demand outstripped supply and that was where the problems started. Anybody who has ever been to a game as big as any semi-final, never mind a final, knows that hundreds or possibly thousands of people will turn up at games like this without tickets. Some buy from touts, some try to steal tickets from other fans and some try to bribe their way in by bunging a steward on a gate. Another well-known tactic is to get a mob together and storm the gates and force the police to get you into the ground to avoid problems outside. It is a tactic that has worked well over the years and one that the police are only too well aware of.

On the day in question, I saw touts getting turned over – and I must say that's no more than they deserve anyway – and I also saw gangs on the lookout for people to turn over in search of tickets. At the Forest end, where the fans were gathering, word was out that there was a gang of Forest fans mobbing up to storm the gates at that end of the ground to gain entry. Everybody was aware that there were hundreds of Liverpool and Forest fans outside without tickets and that there was no way that the police would allow them to roam the streets and possibly stage a running battle around the stadium. When I finally got into the ground I was surprised at how full it was because there were so many people still milling around outside, but the atmosphere at our end was fantastic – loads of singing and all that stuff, and everyone expectant and excited.

I do remember looking up at the other end, as you do, and watching the centre section fill up while the sections at the sides seemed to be comparatively empty, and then thinking that there must be a fight going on, because the police and St Johns were running towards that section. Now, I know that this won't sound nice, but us lot were taunting the Liverpool fans as usual when the messages started to come over the tannoy, and it seemed that one by one we all fell silent and began to watch this disaster unfold.

People soon started to talk about fans getting crushed and killed and others started to drift away as it was obvious that things were bad. It was only in the car on the way home that I even began to realise what I had witnessed, but it didn't seem real. We were more concerned with the replay date and the validity of our tickets for the re-arranged fixture. Down the pub that night my friends were more shocked than I was. There seemed to be a genuine sense of loss and grieving for the people they had seen killed live on television.

As the days passed, we started to get the finger-pointing and accusations in the media, along with detailed diagrams of the stadium and closed-circuit TV pictures of the areas outside the ground before the gates were opened. I watched and waited for someone to stand up and say what had actually happened: that the police had done all they could to control the crowd outside the ground before they were forced to open the gates by people, some with tickets and some without, who were trying to get in. No one stood up and no one was brave enough to say what had happened, not the fictional version, but the truth. Those gates had to be opened – there was no choice at all because people were going to die outside. The tragic mistake was made by those inside who did not realise that they had to filter the incoming fans into the side enclosures.

But the thing that makes me so angry about that day is the reaction from those on Merseyside and in the media. I've spoken to fans from all over the country about Hillsborough – it's one of those subjects that often crops up in conversation when you're talking to supporters – and they all say the same thing: when will someone on Merseyside accept that some of the blame must be taken by those who turned up without tickets? Those people, who came with the specific intention of storming the gates at the Leppings Lane end, just as they had done at many other grounds before, bear as much responsibility for the deaths of those poor Liverpool fans as any police officer present that day, but those words will never be heard.

Liverpool fans are the best in the world, with that cheeky Scouse humour we all know and love. It couldn't be their fault, could it? Well, I'm sorry to say that an awful lot of football fans have lost patience with the calls from Liverpool that heads should roll and that someone should be seen to pay the price for what happened at Hillsborough. Brian Clough was brave enough to say what he felt about the events – and many people forget that he was there after all, and on the pitch – and yet he was slated by the press for saying what he did. Well, the time has come. Hold your hands up, accept a share of the blame and stop pointing the finger in every direction but your own.

Ever since that dreadful day in 1989, Hillsborough has, quite rightly, been discussed by supporters all over the country. At the time, the police took the most horrific amount of criticism for their actions on the day and whatever response they gave was treated with disgust, as if they were attempting to shift the blame. Any attempt by them, or anyone else, to point the finger at the Liverpool fans was seen as trying to blame the victims for their own deaths. The media, the people of Liverpool and the public were quick to join this condemnation of the easiest and most obvious target. There was no way out for the police, they had to take it all, the inquiries, the slurs, anger and frustration at how such a thing could have happened.

The main focus of the attack on the police was that they opened the gates to let people in to the ground. However, many football fans would not describe this decision as total police incompetence, though they do not come out of it totally without blame. Their decision did set in motion a chain of events which was to result in the deaths of almost a hundred people, but it was forced on them by supporters attempting to gain access to the ground without tickets. This has been a common tactic among supporters for some years now and, as the account we included above would suggest, one that was used by both sets of supporters at this game. You can see from the film of Leppings Lane a few minutes before kick-off that a crush was already in existence in the road because of the number of people rushing towards the ground. The police believed that the only way to ease that crush was for them to do what they had done so often before – open the gates. Perhaps, had they insisted that the kick-off was delayed by fifteen minutes, they would have been able to calm the situation. Instead they opened the gates because they felt they had no choice. However, the immediate cause of the disaster was the failure to get the people filtered into the side pens and, when the real crush started, the failure to open the gates on to the pitch quickly enough. However, we will never know how many of those who steamed the gates at the Leppings Lane end actually had tickets to get into the match and, while the police may have got it wrong when dealing with the situation, any supporter who tried to steam the gates helped to cause the problem in the first place and they must carry that with them for the rest of their lives.

The subsequent Taylor Report put forward recommendations that will, hopefully, ensure that such a tragedy will never happen again in this country. You only have to look at the ground improvements taking place at almost every ground in Britain to see that, within stadiums, things are changing for the better. In the main, this has been a good thing for most fans, but there have been a number of unfortunate side-effects which bear directly on supporters, not the least of which is the increase in entrance prices which is driving some people away from watching football altogether, although better facilities are attracting in others. Those who run our national game have failed to address this problem of rising prices. Until they do, they have a long way to go before they have gained the respect of the average supporter.

PART SIX
The Powers That Be

Chapter 13

The Players, the Clubs and the FA

If there's one thing that most supporters love, it's a player who reacts to them. I'm not talking about the hands above the head, patronising clapping reaction to the old 'There's only one . . .', I'm talking about real interaction between a player and the section of the crowd behind the goals, that vociferous mob who can be worth an extra player to any team on a good day. With your own players, the lads you pay to watch week in and week out, it only needs to be a wave, a sly grin or a sneaky gesture to show recognition that we, and what we do, matter and make a difference to the way they perform, and we love it.

At Watford we have a player just like that. I won't mention his name here, but any Watford fan will immediately know who I mean and he's a hero on the terraces. He can be the most frustrating player I've ever seen at times – you know the type, all the talent in the world but he strolls around as if he couldn't care less. But on other occasions, when he turns it on and is really up for it, he's a god. It's not just the class that oozes out of him, it's his response to us, the supporters behind the goal, and he proves that he does indeed care about us. He'll stand in the opposing goalmouth looking at us and waving to gee us up when we're quiet; he shouts and screams at the crowd behind the goal, and when he scores, he goes mental – and it's towards us he heads. He loves it, he loves us and we love him for it, simple as that.

Yes, we know, it's quite pathetic when you think about it in the cold light of day, and it's obvious that he's on a big ego trip, but wouldn't you be the same? Isn't that the dream of all of us? Of course it is – the dream of scoring in front of *your* end and the things that *you* would do; milking the moment, the pure fantasy. Sadly, the FA have ordered the referees to cut down on the celebrations, and that's a crime in itself. Isn't that the reason we all go – the orgasmic thirty seconds among the ninety minutes of mediocrity when we can all go mental?

Of course, while we acknowledge that it's perfectly acceptable for our own players to react to our chanting, if one of the opposing players responds, all hell breaks loose, because that's just not on. The first time I ever experienced this phenomenon was at the Manor Ground when we went with Watford to see what was, if not the last, one of the last games a certain player played for Oxford United before being transferred. From what we could see at the visitors' end, he simply seemed to go through the motions that day. His transfer was almost certain to go through and the last thing he wanted was any sort of injury to take with him, and it appeared that he just did not play to the best of his ability.

Of course, as the visiting fans, we played up to a bloke who was due to move to one of the world's biggest clubs within days and gave him as much verbal as we could – not just because of his transfer but because he didn't look as if he was trying, the ultimate crime to any football supporter. Picture the scene: Oxford are attacking our end and have a corner. This player is standing in the middle of the goalmouth, jigging about as usual, and we are giving him as much verbal as is humanly possible. Suddenly he looks at us, drops his hand behind his back and gives us a quick Harvey Smith. The place goes mental and there's almost a riot as we try to get the attention of either the referee or the police to inform them that a player had abused us, the crowd – disgraceful! Not surprisingly, the ref and the law totally ignore our protestations and so we continue to voice the most indignant outrage for the remainder of the match, which is the catalyst for some subsequent trouble outside, almost certainly because the Oxford fans didn't have a clue what was going on.

Of course, on the way home our indignation turned to good humour because he did exactly what we wanted him to do, and that was to react to us, giving us the excuse to really play up. It wasn't even the gesture in itself that had annoyed us; it was merely that he got away with it. The fact that the whole end had been giving him terrible abuse for over an hour is no excuse; it's personal, and that player has been in the Top 10 of our most disliked players ever since because, like most supporters, we bear a grudge.

That, of course, is the reason supporters abuse footballers, to provoke a reaction, and to the eternal credit of 95 per cent of players, they deal in a positive way with the intimidating chanting hurled at them at some games (if only the crowd could behave in the same manner!). But it is the other 5 per cent in whom we are interested here, because their behaviour can spark off real trouble, just as players fighting on the pitch can cause major problems within the crowd. If you have any doubts whatsoever about such reasoning, there is one single incident which shows just how much effect the actions of either players or supporters can have on the other, and that is the attack on a fan by Eric Cantona. If ever there was an example of how a player's behaviour can provoke supporters, it is this.

We shall not look too deeply into what happened on that January evening in 1995 at Selhurst Park – we have our own opinions just as undoubtedly you have yours, but such was the impact of this incident that it remains clear in the memory to this day. What is certain is that, by his reaction to abuse from a fan, Cantona cost United the Championship and the FA Cup, and any United supporter who denies that is a fool. We would even go as far as to say that Matthew Simmons, the fan in question, did as much to win the silver for Blackburn as Alan Shearer or Kenny Dalglish did, which is surely the ultimate blow for supporter power. However, we are not concerned with that night, but with the snowballing effect it had on the game in general. In this case it was major and ended in tragedy.

Now, we'll probably be accused of being anti-United, but this is certainly not the case. We are no more anti-United than anti any club which does not play at Vicarage Road, but what we are really anti is anything which causes yet more scorn to be poured on to the heads of the average supporter and here United must take some flak. Following Cantona's attack, the game went into shock and suffered the usual onslaught from the media which was soon focused on the supporters. But this time the rest of us came under attack as well, not just the spectators at that game. We were once again portrayed as the right-wing, racist, unemployed thugs so beloved of the British media because *we* had pushed a genius over the edge and possibly out of our game. Within days, popular opinion outside football held that Matthew Simmons had got exactly what he deserved and leaflets and T-shirts giving his address were soon in circulation among United fans, with clear intent. The United media wagon put on its rose-coloured glasses and went on the offensive and 'Just because it's us' became a regular phrase from both the club and the supporters.

With impending court cases and an FA inquiry (another one!), the media were never going to leave this alone for long, but then the worst possible thing happened, as far as the FA were concerned, anyway: United and Palace were drawn in an FA Cup semi-final to be played at Villa Park on Sunday 9 April. Far from sitting back and hoping that the obvious animosity between the fans and the players would vanish in time (in truth it had never really existed until the media bandwagon got involved), the FA now faced the prospect of the two clubs meeting each other in one of the most intense and potentially hostile atmospheres of any game in any season: a Cup semi-final. After a while, the FA got their act together, and, rather than holding their breath and crossing their fingers as is usual, they pointed to this game as an example of a good public relations exercise. To their credit, the match itself did go off peacefully.

Outside the stadium, however, things were different. The

previous encounter ensured that many fans on both sides would indeed indulge in revenge attacks, which is just what happened, and there were a number of minor clashes between fans before the game. However, everything was overshadowed by the unthinkable: the death of a Crystal Palace supporter during a fight outside a Walsall pub. Even now, the circumstances behind this incident are unclear, but it is known that the fans from both clubs had been drinking together quite happily until someone allegedly began to taunt the United supporters about Cantona. Then it all went off, spilling over into the car park, where a fan died.

Football in general was quite rightly outraged at this tragedy, but again, the FA were saddled with the worst possible scenario: the game had to be replayed. In the days after the first game, many concerns were understandably raised in all quarters about when the replay should take place. The police and the FA wanted to get it out of the way as soon as possible, stating that it would have to be played sooner or later, and that having it sooner would give all 'true' fans the chance to pay their respects. Manchester United concurred with this view, while Palace wanted it put back, both as a mark of respect and to give the two sets of supporters the chance to cool down and reflect on what had happened. In the event, the FA overruled Palace and the club took the unusual, but sensible, step of asking their fans not to attend.

The match, of course, attracted great media interest, and all eyes were on the supporters, as one would expect. The police, rather than being sympathetic to the situation, drafted in twice the usual number of officers and stated that they foresaw no problems among the fans, because they were used to dealing with big games at Villa Park. This in itself was a strange response as the majority of problems at the previous match had occurred some distance away from the ground. Players and officials from both clubs appeared on TV requesting that the two sets of supporters put an end to any lingering animosity from the previous encounters and enjoyed the game for what it was – a great sporting contest.

The intense media coverage saw the game start in front of the lowest crowd for an FA Cup semi-final since the war. During the second half, Roy Keane of Manchester United was fouled by a Palace player and it seemed his immediate reaction was to appear to stamp on the player lying below him. Another Palace player, Darren Patterson, ran over and attempted to punch Keane and a mass brawl ensued. All of this happened near the touchline, right in front of supporters whose reaction was to jump to their feet and hurl abuse at those involved. Some were even seen attempting to get on to the pitch to join in. The respect, calm and reverence were shattered in seconds by the very people who had been calling for it.

The subsequent sending-off was viewed with amazement by the player concerned, and some of his team-mates were even seen to offer their condolences as he walked off. The immediate response of both the media and the general public was one of total disgust. The FA, clearly shocked, indicated that those involved would be severely dealt with by the disciplinary board at Lancaster Gate (words we have heard so often before that they hold little meaning), but it was not long before calls for clemency were being made on behalf of all concerned. After all, surely no incident on a pitch was serious enough to merit suspending a player for a Cup final, was it? The aftermath of this incident, in terms of the players' punishments, is pretty irrelevant. What is important is that if you follow the thread, the incident at Selhurst Park in January was an integral link in a sequence of events which included the death of a football supporter. That is an inescapable conclusion, and however much it is denied, there can be no doubt that players' actions can have a direct effect on supporters at the game.

If a visiting player fouls, punches or headbutts a Watford player, he may as well have hit us. It's personal and the reaction will be as hostile as we can make it. While those in and surrounding the directors' box may shake their heads in disgust, they, just like the lads behind the goals, know full well that the atmosphere will immediately change and the game, players and crowd will go up a gear as a result. To state the obvious here, football is indeed a man's game, and while we marvel at the skills of Le Tissier and Hoddle, we all know deep down that, in the English League at least, it is the Hurlocks and the Ruddocks who can win games. Crunching tackles and intimidating defending are as much a part of the English game as the throw-in and the corner. The clubs know that, of course, and managers who scrutinise every second of every game show commendable bias when they claim not to have seen one of their own players almost decapitate an opposing forward right in front of them, whereas they can see that it was 'a certain penalty' on the other side of the pitch. That does not make any of it right, of course. The FA know full well that the behaviour of many players on the pitch is totally unacceptable, and have quite correctly dealt out severe punishments to persistent offenders in the past. Trial by video is certainly here to stay, and I have no doubt that it is an excellent thing because far too many vicious attacks on players have gone unpunished over the last few years.

While the FA are finally getting to grips with things on the pitch, the behaviour of footballers off it is something else, and it is here the FA have been totally ineffective. Like most fans, we have an admiration and grudging respect for all professional footballers, a feeling matched only by our intense jealousy of their lifestyles. As long as they do their best on the pitch, we could not care less what they get up to off it unless it affects us. If a player is homosexual, if he gets caught with someone else's wife, if he has sex with sheep, so what? That just makes him even more interesting; they are only human, after all, and most are as dull as ditchwater. How often have you read a player profile which includes *Minder*, steak and Phil Collins among the answers? We rest our case.

However, when what they get up to starts bringing the game into disrepute, then things take on a different perspective. They inadvertently begin to affect you and me, the supporters, because the non-footballing public begins to believe that our game is rotten, played by thugs and watched by yobs. Throughout the 1994–5 season, we saw footballers and managers accused of, and charged in a court of law with offences that previously would have been unthinkable. The FA have got to take strong action with anyone involved in anything disreputable.

I like to think that 99 per cent of the time I'm a pretty decent sort of bloke. I don't drink at all, nor do I smoke; I don't even clout my kids that often. However, if I were to end up in court accused of hitting someone outside a nightclub or kicking someone in the street, I would feel lucky to get away with a hefty fine and a criminal record. If I attack someone inside a football ground I would expect to be hammered, and if I walked into a police station and admitted that I was a cocaine addict I would expect, at the very least, to have a great deal of pressure put on me to supply the name and addresses of the people who had been selling me the stuff. These things, of course, all happened to players from the Premier League in the 1994–5 season. So what happened? Very little, really. Cantona received a lengthy ban from the FA and community service from the court, a mild punishment considering the fact that he carried out a horrific attack, and in full view of the television cameras, which broadcast the incident throughout the world. Dennis Wise was acquitted on appeal and Paul Merson and Chris Armstrong were simply helped with their problems (although in Merson's case sympathetic treatment was almost certainly the correct action).

To anyone with any sense, this demonstrates only one thing: that footballers can get away with almost anything in British courts. If you are up in front of the magistrate, you would be sentenced there and then. But not players – they have appeals and bail and get to play on for their clubs. Why? The FA, of course, sit back and do little. This is the body of men who fined Vinny Jones £20,000 with a six-month suspended ban for appearing in a video deemed to have brought the game into disrepute, yet when Duncan Ferguson was jailed for head-butting an opponent, there were complaints from within football that players were being targeted by the courts.

While the FA seem apathetic towards violence and drugs, they are positively apoplectic about another issue which has recently been in the news, namely the allegations of 'bungs' involved in the transfers of Scandinavian players to English clubs. So what if someone makes money out of a transfer? As long as the club gets the player it wants, the average fan could not care less. It has little effect on us: we would rather they sorted out the rest of the crap, thanks, than totally preoccupying themselves with where the precious money that *we* put into the game is going.

There was one issue in the news in the same season which sent shivers down the backs of everyone who watches the game, and that was the allegations of players taking bribes. Now, we don't know about you, but we cannot believe that anyone in English football would, or even could, throw a game. We might hear about it in the Far East occasionally, but we refuse to accept that it could happen here. There is one simple reason for that view; we do not want to believe it, or even to contemplate that any player at any level could let down both his team-mates and the supporters merely to fill his own bank account. We will refuse to accept that it could happen in England until someone tells us that they actually did it. That, to us, would be the ultimate kick in the teeth, and would mean the end of the game as far as we're concerned.

Of course, all the things we have talked about have only one interest to us, and that is their influence on supporters, but many of them are pretty minor. We know that if the players play up on the pitch then, to a certain extent, so will we, and we know that if a player has been a naughty boy then we will give him plenty of abuse for it. But at the end of the day, so what? Don't all these things just add spice to the game? It is easy for us to sit here and say things like that because we're old enough to understand why players do what they do, but there is a group of people who are influenced by the actions of players and that is children. Kids, both boys and girls, love football, and thank Christ for that; it means the game is in safe hands. The lad who comes to my house every week to collect my pools coupon is no more than eight, but he's a season-ticket holder at Vicarage Road and his whole family never misses a game. Come the

Thursday, he is still talking about the result of the previous home game as if it had finished twenty minutes ago. Thank goodness for that, because no matter what your views on families at matches, the fact that kids of his age are as in love with the game as us is a wonderful thing for football.

In the aftermath of the Cantona affair and the attendant mud-slinging at everyone except our Eric, much was made of the effect that his behaviour – or that of any professional player, for that matter – could have on young kids. Although I shrugged this off at the time, I have recently begun watching a few junior games and have seen children in their Liverpool and Man United shirts, hacking players down, hurling abuse and throwing punches. Just a thought.

For many clubs, attracting kids and families to games is essential because of the revenue they bring in. Much the same can be said for the growth of mobs. It is the addition of the new, younger members to replace those packing it in which ensures the continued survival of a hard-won reputation. The establishment, and subsequent popularity, of the Premier League have begun to have a serious side-effect in terms of football violence and the mob culture, and it is one we need to examine. At many clubs in the Premier League, it is now almost impossible to get a match ticket. In many cases, they are allocated either in rotation or by lottery. This means that a great many people do not manage to get to the games they want to see, and this can have disastrous consequences for the numbers who want to travel together. Similarly, the people who hold season tickets at clubs where sell-outs are a regular occurrence are unable to secure the same privilege for their kids, and so the average age of the crowd looks likely to gradually increase over the seasons. This will ensure that the mobs will cease to be linked to certain clubs. Moreover, a great many mobs will not have a game to see on Saturday because their game has been moved to Sunday to accommodate live television. So just what happens when you get a mob who cannot go and watch their team for some reason? Just what do they do? They travel to alternative matches, of course, and cause trouble there, or they form an alliance with a club from a lower division and fight with both home and visiting supporters.

Many supporters have gone to other games and caused trouble when their matches have been cancelled while they were en route, but we are now coming across many cases of mobs from big clubs turning up at First Division games or large firms hitting not just clubs or grounds, but town centres for absolutely no reason other than that they wanted a rumble. This is obviously a very dangerous phenomenon indeed, because sooner or later we will see a mob which, although they have sworn allegiance to a certain club, rarely if ever actually see them play. We already know of a large group from a major Premier League club who have accepted that they will never all get tickets together and instead meet, as a group, in a pub on matchdays to watch or listen to the game on television or radio. Just how long will it be before the next step is taken there? If the travel bug bites, the result could be very scary indeed.

The letter below came to us from a supporter in the West Country who wishes to remain anonymous. The content leaves you in little doubt as to the writer's opinions on the way the game is being promoted and run by those in charge, but it also poses many questions that supporters up and down the country ask on a regular basis. As football becomes more and more business-orientated, many fans are indeed finding themselves alienated, angry and ready to fight back or even turn away from the game altogether. It really would be difficult to find another industry which takes so much from its customers yet pays so little attention to their thoughts and needs as football does. For some, football's commercialism is having an alienating effect; one which could even provoke violence. It is certainly an issue that could become increasingly important.

A Fan's Rant

Me? I was tear-gassed in Turin, run by Millwall at *that* game at L*t*n, have seen a young girl have her cheek taken off by a half-brick thrown by a QPR fan and have been scared shitless up and down the country for years. I'm no anorak, either – I know the score and have certainly been about, but I just got so sick of it all I decided to grow up and get out. It was only then that I realised how much I loved watching football. I used to be a season-ticket-holding, membership-card-carrying supporter and remember the great days when my team avoided relegation on the last day of the season and was worshipped by the fans. Well, even they can all fuck off now. Professional footy is shit.

Why do you stand for being ripped off and treated like sheep? I just don't like being some sod's cash cow. It really fucks me off when I hear that it costs £12 to see Notts County. Do I really have to explain to another human being why that sucks so badly it is almost surreal? How can some bloke who works himself stupid all week trying to buy trainers for his kids – *if* he's lucky enough to have a job in the first place – afford that? Why are you paying that much? I'll tell you why, it's because pro footballers are a bunch of thieving donkeys who, along with their agents, have stolen your game from right under your noses.

Anyone I see walking about with a club shirt with the name 'Barnes' or 'Sutton' on his back, should, in a perfect world, be shot in the street. If you're reading this and you've done it yourself – grow up, you thick bastard. If you pay £3 for a programme; if you think it's good that the FA have sold the family silver to such an extent that even the national team wears a kitmaker's logo bigger than the team badge; if you think it's a good thing for the League Cup to be coated in Coca-Cola ribbons and lifted to the tune 'It's the real thing'; if you just have to have this week's Man United shirt; if you just have to dial 0898 numbers to get the latest news of your own team – well, you're as big a twat as the rest of them. I hope you end up in a Freight Rover-sponsored hell with Beelzebub, brought to you in association with Zetters, who sticks a fork with 'Live on Sky' on the handle up your arse.

The pragmatist will tell you that 'we have to compete

with the rest of Europe' or moan about affording new stadiums. Bollocks. Small clubs are going to the wall for the price of an executive box at Highbury, that's the reality. The stupid thing about it all is that the FA think that they are being so smart, so managerial, so go-getter. Well, let me ask you this. When you see sport from the USA, the land of the fast buck, do you see shirts with sports sponsorship? Is the Superbowl 'in association with Kentucky Fried Chicken'? Is the World Series about to become the M & M's Trophy? No, because the Americans, who are the world leaders in marketing, realise that in the long term it cheapens the product, alienates the fans and reduces the spectacle to something meaningless, devoid of tradition and dignity.

I even think that one of the reasons behind the resurgence of thuggery around the game has been the increasing commercialism of the sport. The game has always been a perfect mirror of the real world, one that is perhaps meaningful to ordinary people. It has its wars, its leaders, its heroes, its crises, its villains and its scandals. It's big, it's global, and everyone wants to win, but, unlike the real world, when you win, you get to gloat about it till the next one comes along. Hardly surprising, then, that the problems of the real world are moving back into football: gang warfare, racism and apathy towards the person standing next to you. The professional game has become Football plc in order to pay some players obscene amounts of money per week, and that money comes from you, and everyone like you. The game is cheapened; it's not so special any more. It's getting more like the *Gladiators* every week and the FA cannot or will not stop it.

You don't have to be unemployed to be a football thug, or live in an inner-city high-rise, or be the product of a one-parent family. You just need to be in a rut; simply pissed off with living in a country where you're disenfranchised and have little or no say in decisions which directly affect you, and sick of being told that saying you're proud to be English means you're not far short of being a Nazi.

You just have to be totally fucked off with a government selling off the country to anyone who has a few quid, with seeing the place you live in and its culture disintegrate before your very eyes, and to feel cheated by the bastards who've done it. We would all love to have respect for the law but we can't, because they don't protect us, they protect the people who are oppressing us. So we take solace in football – but even that is being sold off in the same sad way, bit by bit, and the people who will suffer most are the people who have no voice: the fans. The so-called experts miss the point. We're pissed off and we want to kick back, have an effect. We want our game back and we want to know why they've sold our sport from under our feet, and why it costs more than ever to watch it.

Are you reading this in Lancaster Gate? If so, then stick your executive-match-ball-sponsored-in-association-with-brought-to-you-by shit up your arse. You've let the supporters down and if you want to look at why some pillocks are actually killing each other at some feeding frenzy of a Cup semi-final, then have a look at your own greed and the way you've robbed us of something *we* used to own. Give us something back, something worthy of the beautiful game, before there's nothing left to recommend it to the next generation.

The next account is the result of a long and very interesting conversation with a tout outside Wembley Stadium. It is placed here because it gives an insight into part of the business side of football that is rarely discussed – ticket allocation and distribution. For obvious reasons it is anonymous, but it also gives a good insight into a group of people who are much abused but on whom many people rely.

A Tout's View

I'm a ticket tout. That's not a confession or anything, it's just what I do. I don't deal in just football – I'll sell or get any ticket for anyone – but you will find me at every Wembley event and outside the biggest game in the capital every Saturday. Most people think that we're all part of the same organisation, working for one guy who creams off all the money, but that just ain't the case. I work on my own – I always have and always will – and although there are a couple of big crews out there, most touts work independently. The regulars at games up and down the country will know their faces by now. There is, however, one thing we all do, and that's look out for each other, either keeping an eye out for the law or watching for potential trouble.

We all know the feelings about ticket touts in this country. Most people think we're one step down from cockroaches, but all we're trying to do is earn a living. You might not like it, but that's what we do. Despite what people feel about us, I think that there is a grudging respect for us and I have to say that we don't get anything like the problems you would expect. I think that there are a few reasons for that. At the end of the day, people know that if they are desperate, they can get a ticket for any game from a tout. Ask yourself whether you have ever been glad to see one of us at a big game. Course you have. I know that sometimes we charge way over the odds, but it's supply and demand. Many's the time I've ended up either giving tickets away or selling them for less than half the face value. That's the way it goes.

What you should be asking yourself is how we get hold of all those tickets that the genuine fans never seem to be able to get, especially for the big games. Now, I'm not going to tell you the answer to that because I've got a family to feed and contacts to protect, but what I will say is that, in my opinion, football does not belong to the fans any more. It's all down to corporate business. How many fans who actually support the teams involved do you think get to see the Cup final? Put it another way: how many people who, on any other day would be out playing golf or shopping *do* get to see the biggest game of the season? Did you see how many well-dressed women and kids were at Wembley for the Man United v Everton final? Bloody thousands, and I bet they didn't queue at Old Trafford in the pouring rain for their tickets, either – that's if they even know where it is. That might give you a clue as to where and how I get most of my tickets. We know fans hate to see us outside grounds, but the same people are more than happy to use us if they're desperate, and I can honestly say that if it wasn't for us, there would be a lot of empty seats on Cup final day.

Another question you should consider is how all these ticket agencies come across more tickets than I can ever hope to get my hands on, and what about the handling charge they stick on top? That can be up to £2.50 for a Wembley ticket, and that's a lot of money when you add up 80,000 possible punters. Really, you fans are mugs anyway when it comes to tickets. At Wembley you can't take a ticket back for a refund if you don't use it, and that goes for any game I've ever been at, for that matter. Why is that? What about the bloke who turns up at a game with a spare ticket because his mate can't come or his kid's got chickenpox? What does he do? Well, I'll tell you what he should do, he should either rip it up, give it away or look for a tout he recognises who might buy it from him so that at least he'll get something back.

Of course, he could try to sell the ticket himself, but then he'd wide open to trouble which will start the second he finds out that the bloke he's just sold it to is an undercover copper who then arrests him for touting. I have actually seen a bloke on Wembley Way, with two kids, who was holding his hand in the air trying to sell a spare ticket when the Filth moved in and nicked him, leaving the two kids bawling their eyes out on their own! When I went over to try to help him out by explaining that he wasn't a real tout, all the coppers said was that they'd heard it all before and started to drag him off! Luckily for him, some other supporters managed to get him away, but this is something that is going to happen more and more with these new laws.

The thing is that the police won't be able to stop us anyway, and they know it. We know the rules. So they will just turn to the easy targets like the bloke I just mentioned, or the other odd supporters, just to justify their presence. The law, like the game, doesn't give a shit about the fan, that's for sure.

Of course, one of the worst things about being a tout is that there's always the chance that you'll get turned over. Luckily that's only happened to me once, and that was at Wembley a few years ago. A load of Liverpool fans turned over loads of touts, not just me. I lost a lot of money that day, and now I think twice about selling when there's a Scouse team playing. But I know that the big crew who run touting in Liverpool were decidedly unhappy about what happened to us that day, and I heard that they paid a few people back over it. Most of the touts who were turned over, me included, have recouped their money over the years by selling to Scousers at higher prices than to anyone else.

There's no doubt about it, being a tout is a risky way to earn a living and it's bloody hard work sometimes but I do genuinely feel that we are offering a service to fans, and maybe you should think about that the next time you're locked out of a game.

Chapter 14
The Power of the Press

This country has some of the finest sports reporters in the world, of that there can be no doubt whatsoever. In the press and on television, our sports coverage is far superior to anything else we have seen throughout the world, and the explosion of sports, particularly football, on the satellite channels has been nothing short of spectacular. However, the standard of sports reporting is not something that we are too concerned with here; what we will explore is the media reaction to the problem of football violence.

We believe that the role of a free press should be to provide the facts behind any given argument, allowing the reader or viewer to make up his or her own mind. If this basic rule is not followed, you will find that being presented with only one viewpoint leads Mr and Mrs Average to believe that it is the truth. If you have any doubt about that, just look at television in Russia, Algeria or China, to name just three, where control of the media leads to control of the state. We are not saying that Britain is a totalitarian state, by any means (and we are certainly not advocating it!) but it has been all too easy for the media in the past to present the viewpoint they wanted to put over without giving access to anybody wishing to respond or disagree. Coverage of football violence is a classic case in point.

Newspaper reporters have a job to do. They have to sell their papers. They do that by writing about specific events, news, current affairs or sport, in such a way that we, the public, want to read about them and will buy their paper as opposed to any other. That may be simplistic, but it forms the basis of their role. Not many reporters are lucky enough to have stories fall into their laps every day of the week, and so they have to go looking for, or will be sent to find, something to fill the pages. There are many safe bets for a good story – the royals, celebrities, the odd spectacular criminal case, that sort of thing – but not long ago football violence was high up on any editor's list.

Let's give a hypothetical scenario to see how they approach the subject: England are playing an away game. The paper sends a news (not sports) reporter with the fans on the pretext of seeing how they are treated, but in reality he is going to see what the group get up to. As in so many such cases, nothing happens – or if it does, it involves either the group being attacked by some of the home fans or is no more than a minor argument. Nothing too serious there, but before you know it, the papers back home are full of 'England fans shame country again!'-type stories. Of course, as anyone who has travelled with England will tell you, this is not a hypothetical situation at all, because it has happened, not just once but many times. During the seventies and eighties, stories of England fans taking part in pitched battles or riots or being deported were all over the papers, which presented the participants as 'Steve from Bristol' or 'John, a Chelsea fan'. Television film of these lads coming back to Heathrow from away games showed them boasting of their exploits to anyone who would listen, but how many interviews did they have to do to get someone to say exactly what they wanted to hear?

The way that all sections of the media portrayed football fans at the time led to the assumption that everyone who went to football was a practising hooligan, because the people who did not go to matches – Mr and Mrs Average, if you like – were seeing nothing but negative coverage, and that's what they took to be the norm. The account of England playing in Germany which we shall come to shortly is Dougie's, and gives the truth

of what happened on that night. The way the press behaved –
two newspapers in particular, and we have never bought either
of them since – was beyond appalling; it was disgraceful. The
way we were depicted on that night was as drunken thugs out
to destroy this country's reputation abroad. The truth was that
the English fans were attacked and provoked beyond belief,
and you can only take so much of this before you respond. The
fact that this took place in Germany, perceived as England's
oldest enemy, was immaterial; it could have been anywhere.
What happened was that events before and after the game,
incitement from the British press and provocation by the police
and German fans combined to result in a catastrophic outbreak
of violence.

We should not be too surprised at the sensationalist way the
press have reported violence in this country, because it is by no
means new. As far back as the fifties, when mods and rockers were
rioting on the south coast, media coverage of their exploits led to
copycat incidents throughout the country within weeks. Exactly
the same thing happened with the skinheads who, in the sixties,
were merely lads just out of borstal who were shunned by society.
One report of a skinhead gang in London, and suddenly they
were all over the country. Again, the press coverage inspired
copycat behaviour. Football violence was no different, as widespread media stories about the trouble during the seventies led to
club after club suddenly finding themselves with a problem they
were unable, or unwilling, to deal with. Mobs of travelling fans,
descending on towns throughout England every Saturday afternoon, precipitated panic measures by the clubs and some harsh
policing methods were introduced in a vain attempt to control a
problem that was, by then, already out of control. There can be no
doubt that the media had a significant input into the spread of the
football mob culture during that period, and their influence on
this subject continues.

Thankfully, things are very different these days. Although the
regional press still carries plenty of reports into the exploits of
football groups, the national press tends to ignore the day-to-
day stuff because, in general, at club level anyway, it isn't really

newsworthy any more. However, when there is a major incident, the press still go to town and we are bombarded with graphic images of bloody faces, police constraining men in armlocks and even blond-haired Irish kids staring blankly into space (we hate that bloody picture). But to be fair, a great deal of the reporting in the 'sensible' newspapers is far more responsible than in previous years. Certainly, where English supporters abroad have taken a hammering, sections of the media have, quite rightly, been highly critical of the foreign authorities and treatment of our fans (pre-Dublin, anyway) has been positive.

The tabloids, of course, are a different matter entirely. They relish the chance to wheel out their ridiculous headlines (you know the sort of thing: NIGHT OF SHAME, NOT AGAIN!, IT'S ONLY A GAME!) and, as all supporters know, merely sensationalise the violence rather than explore the real issues involved. We have always found it strange that certain tabloids, while putting themselves forward as 'the people's newspapers', take great delight in slagging off a section of the public for whom they purport to be publishing and who all too often receive abusive and violent treatment abroad. Very odd.

Television is another medium which has been guilty of provocative reporting in the past. Flashing up pictures of supporters rioting to illustrate a report about English fans leads to an immediate association that 'English fan' and 'hooligan' are synonymous. But as we all know, this is not always the case at all. Reports of drunken English yobs patrolling foreign streets are thankfully becoming rarer, but they still occur, despite the fact that in most countries it would be a highly dodgy thing to do, and most supporters are anything but stupid. Similarly, almost every documentary on the subject over the years has been woefully inaccurate in its research, particularly as regards organised groups, and has merely succeeded in glorifying the very subject it has attempted to condemn. Nearly every supporter will remember the television play The Firm, which portrayed a firm of 'Cockney' thugs. While laughable in some aspects, it was probably the closest thing to the truth we have ever seen on British TV, which some would say is quite a sad reflection on the accuracy of their drama.

Yet, while it is important to remember that in general the number of large-scale incidents at games has decreased, it is clear, as we have stressed already, that the problem has not gone away; it has merely moved its theatre. Go to any match in the country and you will pick up the rumours – 'such-and-such a mob did this', or 'Did you hear about this mob taking that pub?' – and it should be remembered that there is no smoke without fire. The efforts of a great many people have brought us a good distance down the road towards ridding football of this problem once and for all, but there is still a long way to go and the press have one of the most important roles in deciding how fast we will get there.

England

It must have been back in 1986–7. I'm sure of that, because at the time I was in the forces serving in Germany and we were looking forward to the European Championships which were to be held in 1988. It was the first time I'd ever been to an England game abroad, and there was a great deal of concern about the behaviour of the British servicemen at the game – so much so that for a time it was planned to make tickets unavailable to the forces. As it was, all the servicemen attending the game were given strict orders and told in no uncertain terms what would happen to us if anyone became involved in any trouble.

The game itself was held in Düsseldorf, not far from the Dutch border, and I was on a coach full of servicemen who followed clubs from all over the UK. There were even a few Jocks along just for the crack. When we arrived at the stadium, which, like most German grounds, is superb, we were unloaded away from the ground and told to walk down through all the car parks. Along the way, we met various groups of lads from England who kept telling us that it had been going off all day and all over the place already because the locals and the *Polizei* were trying it on.

As is usual in these cases, these little groups were starting to mob together for protection. A group of German fans had just steamed through one of the car parks, damaged a few British cars and dealt out a few slaps, but they had done the off before they encountered any real opposition.

There was the added complication that some of the Brits were totally skint and had been taking money from tabloid journalists to stage fights and throw the odd brick for the cameras. At that time, football violence was really big news and the majority of the hacks at the game had nothing to do with the sports pages. Instead they wanted to report on how much trouble the English fans had caused, and of course, they couldn't report that there wasn't any, could they? The atmosphere outside the ground was hostile to say the least, and just after we passed through the main car park it all went off behind us. Whether the German mob had come back or not I don't know, but the police went streaming through us towards it, batons flying, and a few of our lads got a wallop, which did not go down too well. It was obvious that after the game all hell was going to break loose, a situation that was not helped by one of Bobby Robson's team's less successful performances.

They kept us in for a while after the game, but a lot of the English lads were well drunk by then and had been getting a lot of grief from the police during the match. This served only to inflame an already bad situation. The locals had seen enough and were off as fast as they could move, so any trouble was coming from the police. Other rivalries had surfaced as well: the animosity between the Army and the Air Force lads was getting very heated by this time and had resulted in at least one bloke getting a good kicking in the toilets. The great north–south divide was also rearing its head as a number of Londoners conducted a slanging match with a group of Scousers.

Before long the atmosphere was one of total hatred – and it was getting worse by the second. The stadium staff then decided that they did not want any of this and let us leave,

which we did, only to come face to face with a line of
baton-wielding riot police, the smallest of whom looked to
be about 7 feet tall. It was so obvious that they wanted it to
go off it was embarrassing, and with the English lads at
fever pitch, they didn't have to wait long. All the rival
English factions had suddenly closed ranks, because, as far
as they were concerned, this was fighting for their country,
they had a reputation to uphold and they had to prove to
these wankers that they would not be turned over by any
bastard. A group of about twenty just steamed across the
car park, closely followed by about another hundred, and
the police just ran, leaving this mob stranded.

It was then that the horses came in behind them and just
trampled or clubbed anything they could reach. They
pulled out and the riot police came back in to do the
nicking, as well as dishing out some serious damage to a
good few of our lads. Afterwards, we had to admit that it
was a bloody good tactic; it had caught the mob out completely, but only because the remainder of the crowd held
back. Otherwise it could have been a nightmare for them.
Funnily enough, after that it all went flat. I suppose seeing
loads of your 'mates' getting a good hiding tends to calm
you down a little.

Of all the times I've been to football, that night was one of
the worst, for two reasons. The first is that a lot of people
were badly hurt, and although quite a few of them
deserved what they got, many were totally unconnected
with what was going on. The second was that the atmosphere was unlike anything I had ever felt before (or since).
It was just total hatred, and it was scary. In the British press
the next day, the English supporters were denounced as the
scum of the earth. The photographs and TV pictures were
edited in such a way as to make it out to be all our fault, but
anyone who was there will know the truth: that the press
and the police were so desperate for it to go off that they
actually caused it all. The police wanted to prove they
could handle it and the British press wanted a story.

Bad press coverage is not confined to distorted reporting and manufacturing stories. Another aspect of this topic is the reverse treatment: many incidents abroad are ignored or hardly mentioned in the media. During Euro '88, for example, there was a major incident of crowd violence of which many people in this country were unaware. The letter below was sent by Darren from Bolton, who witnessed it.

Hamburg

Over the years I have become increasingly annoyed at the way in which the violence of the English fans during Euro '88 was reported in this country. Anyone who attended the England games would admit that the usual heavies were in attendance, and that they did do the odd bit of business here and there, but what was not reported was that the British press were paying people, including German skinheads, 100 marks to drape themselves in a Union Jack and throw bricks through windows just to get the pictures they wanted. Another thing they 'inadvertently missed' was the violence of the German and Dutch fans at all of their games. Most annoying of all was the way the British press almost totally ignored the riot that took place after the semi-final between the host nation and the Dutch in Hamburg.

After England had been knocked out, we found ourselves left with tickets for both semi-finals, the first of which meant a long trip to Hamburg. We decided to hire a car and take our time driving up rather than go by train. We didn't know it at the time, but that was probably the best decision we ever made. When we arrived in Hamburg about three hours before the game, the city seemed very quiet, which was not what we had expected at all – we were all convinced that there would be trouble. You know what it's like, you can feel it when there's a big game about to happen, but here there was none of that – the place was dead.

We parked the car and made our way to the bar where all

the English fans had arranged to meet. We had planned to mob up and have a pop at the Dutch and Germans, but many of the lads had gone home instead. I think that secretly they just did not fancy this one at all – it was clearly going to be only for the brave.

As kick-off got closer, some of the lads decided to sell their tickets and stay in the bar to watch the match on television. We decided to go as we had come all this way, so we dived in the car and drove to the ground. The car park and stadium were surrounded by woodland and the atmosphere was like one big party, with people having picnics or playing football, that sort of thing. People kept coming up to us, but it was only to shake hands and say, 'Bad luck to you English.' It was quite a laugh, really.

When we got into the ground, we found that we were in a section of German fans right next to the Dutch supporters. Also in our bit were loads of skinheads, and I must say that they looked like the biggest load of tossers I have ever seen. As you would expect, we took the piss out of them right through the game with no comeback at all, but it was an education to see the two sets of fans giving each other the big 'un, so different from the way we do it over here.

The game itself had passed off with no trouble at all when, with one minute to go, the Dutch scored. All of a sudden, the atmosphere changed completely. The Dutch were taking the piss and the Germans going mental, and we suddenly went very quiet indeed. After the final whistle, we decided to hang back for a while and watch the Dutch lads celebrate, which was not a pretty sight, really. The Germans, in the meantime, were looking well pissed off as they left the ground; seriously unhappy.

After about fifteen minutes we got bored with watching all that orange dancing about so we left the stadium and walked towards the car park, keeping very quiet and wearing that 'We're pissed off, we lost' face that most footy fans learn to put on after a few dodgy moments at away games. As we walked along, we were joined by loads of Germans who had been walking through the woods. Soon we found ourselves in the middle of quite a large group of blokes, all of whom were not happy Hermans. Up ahead, we could see crowds of the Dutch fans singing and dancing around their coaches, and as we walked into the car park the Germans at the front were starting to deal out a few slaps. The police were nowhere to be seen and this was looking ugly.

Suddenly, there was a long blast on a horn and about six or seven flares shot into the sky and lit up the whole car park. It was obviously a prearranged signal for it all to go off. I must say that I have never seen such a well-organised hit in my entire life. The Dutch did not have a chance as the Germans totalled the coaches and any vehicle in that park without German number plates. Some were dragging people out of cars and kicking the shit out of them, while others were throwing anything they could find. All those Germans, with the stupid haircuts they have – you know, short on top and long at the back – were going totally berserk.

We got out of there as quickly as we could, got back to our car and locked the doors, but there were Germans everywhere and within minutes we were surrounded. However, thanks to the German plates, they left us alone. Some of them started shouting at us and it was not hard to work out that they wanted us out of the car to join in the fun. I think that without a doubt it was the only time I have ever been glad to be mistaken for anything but an Englishman. We just sat there pretending to be pissed off at 'our' team's defeat and we got away with it.

The police just seemed to let it all happen. They did not show up in the car park at all, and the German fans just kept at it for what seemed like an hour but was probably only about ten minutes. When we eventually got the car moving and reached the exit, we saw that the riot vans were actually waiting outside. When they saw this, the German mob steamed past us and went for them. One of the riot vans got turned over and was set on fire and the police quickly withdrew, leaving a situation that was rapidly getting out of hand. This mob had lost control of it all completely and were taking out anything they could. As for us, we were shitting it. We got away from there as quickly as we could. Thank Christ they never knew we were English.

The obvious thing to do would have been to leave for home, but like all blokes in Hamburg, we had to go to the Reeperbahn, the red-light district for which Hamburg is famous. As we arrived, we saw hundreds of riot police who, like us, were certain that there would be a lot more trouble before the night was over, so we drove around and found a bar full of Irish fans who had been watching the game there all night and parked our car right outside. After about twenty minutes, we heard the German fans coming down the road, but this time they were accompanied by hordes of riot police walking alongside them. The Irish fans were sitting outside this bar, singing away like they do, and as soon as the Germans saw them, that was it. Every window went in as they steamed into the Irish lads, who didn't have a clue what was going on. The pub and the Irish lads were wrecked, yet once again, the police did almost nothing to stop it. I'm sure that someone was watching over us that night, because our car was unmarked despite all this. It did not have a single scratch on it!

The rest of the night saw this mob roaming around the red-light district at will, smashing the odd window and generally giving the police a hard time. Not surprisingly, we didn't see many Dutch fans celebrating that night. Mind you, we didn't see much about it in the British papers either. Funny, that.

Chapter 15
The Police

If there is one subject that causes emotions to run high at football, it is the subject of the police. Almost everyone to whom we spoke when compiling this book had experience of their methods, and it has to be said that not all of them have been very good. Crowd control inside grounds these days is generally getting better due to the increased power of the stewards, and the use of closed-circuit television has done a great deal to eradicate violence. However, their methods outside grounds can sometimes leave a lot to be desired, as can the performance of some of their officers, a matter to which we shall return later.

Although trouble within grounds has existed since the birth of the game itself, things started to get serious in the sixties, when football saw the advent of large numbers of travelling fans due to the availability of relatively cheap and readily available transport. The youth of the time saw football as the ideal outlet for their aggressions; something to supplement, and in some cases replace, the mods-and-rockers trend that was so high profile during that period. People, particularly young men, soon discovered the attraction of the terraces and the associated camaraderie and became hooked. Travelling away with their clubs became a way of life for many and provided the ideal opportunity for them to show exactly what they were made of and to prove that their club, town or county were the very best. While conflict at most games became the norm for many young men, there were certain matches at which it became almost compulsory. The north–south divide afforded plenty of scope for trouble up and down the country, but the local derby games provided the chance to prove that your group were the top boys in your local area, be it in singing, drinking or fighting, and this soon resulted in some major incidents at football grounds all over England.

In the 'good old days' of football violence, the seventies and early eighties, the way the police dealt with what was, at times, a horrific problem inside the grounds was to flood the area and nick as many people as possible, an approach which usually resulted in making a bad situation even worse, as no self-respecting mob would let any of its members be arrested. In my own experience, searching was, to say the least, random and I can well remember walking across the Shed at Stamford Bridge tripping over an assortment of weapons that would have supplied a small African nation. As the police continued to blame football for this problem and football continued to blame society, policing strategy evolved and stricter segregation and a more heavy-handed approach were adopted. This method was all well and good, but problems arose when some of the more enthusiastic officers attempted to enforce the rules to the very letter. In the process, they alienated not only the football hooligan but also the genuine supporter he or she was attempting to protect. This, again, had a negative effect: it caused almost all supporters to look upon the police as a second enemy, sometimes even the first, especially at away games. The powers that be did nothing to defuse the situation, so it worsened and incidents became more frequent.

It was a vicious circle. The police began to treat all supporters as hooligans and the media coverage of football gave them the chance to show their efficiency by dealing rapidly with incidents that, in some cases, they themselves had provoked by their aggressive behaviour. The introduction of fences, strict and often overbearing policing and the appalling facilities at most grounds led the average fan to feel, and then to behave, like an animal. Looking back now, it is quite incredible that we used to actually look forward to paying out our own hard-earned money to stand out in the open, served by catering that was, at best, appalling and toilets that would have got the average restaurant closed down. The planned adoption of identity cards and banning of away fans were laughable attempts to control it all, and the fact that neither was successful shows that panic measures were being sought by the football establishment, the government and the police. The creation by the police of football intelligence units (a contradiction in terms, some thought,) was possibly a step in the right direction, but the use of undercover officers (such as those involved in the infamous Operation 'Own Goal') at anything other than the big clubs was a mistake. This attempt at infiltrating the mobs turned out to be a high-profile blunder. We have met at least one group of supporters who had been infiltrated by an undercover copper, sussed the guy and had fed the police false, and in some cases completely contrary, information for an entire season.

The fact that the media dedicated such a volume of newsprint to the few court cases that arose out of these operations was held up by the authorities as an indication of their success. Yet the opposite was almost certainly true. The one simple step that neither football nor the police took, the one thing that would possibly – no, probably – have helped them in their search for a solution, was to ask the fans for their opinions and their assistance. Instead, the football establishment looked upon all supporters with the same disdain, and the police viewed them all as potential criminals. It was a classic case of tarring everyone with the same brush, and a terrible mistake. The police then started to exert a major influence on the staging of games. Early kick-offs, pubs closing, Sunday matches and, in the case of Cup games, even changes of venue, became a routine and accepted police tactic and one that continues to this day.

The one event that changed the face of football forever was a tragedy, Hillsborough. Much has been written about what happened on that fateful day in 1989, but the fact that it happened at all proves that the great game in Britain had allowed itself to deteriorate to such an extent that it was treating the most important people of all, the fans, appallingly. It was only after Hillsborough that football realised what it had become and the fans themselves began to ask what was going on within the game. The fact that our opinions were canvassed and acted upon proved to be a turning point, because it proved that we were important to the game – we are, of course, its greatest asset: its customers. However much you agree or disagree with the feelings of the Taylor Report, there is no doubt at all that the vast majority of grounds these days are cleaner, kinder and safer places to be.

The introduction of CCTV, funded by the Football Trust, proved to be the most valuable tool in the campaign against violence inside grounds during the late eighties and early nineties. The fact that the participants could be quickly targeted and arrested, either at the ground or at a later date, was seen as a development that would strike fear into the people who planned these acts. This is exactly what it achieved, and violence on the pitched-battle scale within stadiums vanished, apparently forever. However, events during the 1994–5 season have since shown that the problem of pitch invasions has possibly returned, which indicates that CCTV, like segregation before it, is no longer the powerful weapon it once was. People are becoming braver and are realising that if they are not arrested on the day, then they are highly unlikely to be arrested in a dawn raid merely for running on to the pitch. Crowd safety in football grounds is an area the authorities should look at very closely once again, in case the problem returns.

Despite the great strides made in crowd monitoring, the attitudes of the police on the ground have not been so quick to change and the power-crazed tinpot dictators we all know and love are still prevalent within stadiums at all levels. Do these people not realise that we, as taxpayers, expect them not only to uphold the law, but also to foster respect for it? This cannot be done by someone behaving like a fascist in front of a stand full of people on a Saturday afternoon, or refusing to carry out the requests of the very people he has been assigned to protect. For example, I have twice recently witnessed small groups of opposing fans coming into the home end, our end, despite highly visible and vocal warnings from the club that they would be ejected if caught. If a group of supporters does that then they are trying to provoke trouble – it's as simple as that. On both these occasions, the police and stewards were alerted by home fans; on both occasions they did nothing and violence erupted. This resulted in unnecessary arrests and negative coverage in the media, but to me the worst aspect was the impression it made on those visiting the ground for the first time. As far as they were concerned, nothing had changed. Football has now lost these people forever due entirely to the police and stewards failing to respond to the situation.

If anti-hooligan measures have been swiftly developed and implemented at stadiums themselves, outside them things are moving at a snail's pace. The clubs and constabularies may well say that they take huge steps to accommodate the wishes of the travelling fan these days, but in reality this has little effect on the potential troublemakers. If a mob wants trouble it will find trouble, and it is here that the police are really up against it. Many people like to visit other towns, have a drink and go to football in the afternoon, and there is nothing wrong with that. The problem is that in doing this as a group of blokes, you usually face two hurdles. The first is the police, because as far as many of them are concerned, if you're a group of blokes, you're after trouble. So you get hauled up to the ground early or, worse, down to the nick until the game is over – just in case. The second is the home fans. This is an understandable problem, because we are all the same when we're at home: the visiting fan is an extension of the visiting team, and clearly we want to beat them. As we have already seen here, as an away fan you are an obvious target, and this fact is accepted by both sides. It is not a nice situation, but it is accepted because there is nothing you can do about it. Either you don't go, or you go mobbed up, or you are very careful.

The police, meanwhile, know who their local mob are and where they will be, but rarely seem to deal with them first. The police attitude to the travelling fan in England leaves much to be desired. There is one example which clearly highlights the fact that people react according to the way they are treated. Before the European Championships in Germany in 1988, the British media had convinced the entire country that World War Three was due the second the English arrived, and it has to be said that a great deal of planning had been carried out by the big firms to ensure that they were not disappointed. However, the police in Germany had it completely sussed. Their policy was one of containment. At each game they allocated, and then kept us in, one or two streets and let us drink in the bars there to our hearts' content. They knew exactly where we were and were generally friendly and very helpful, and so we behaved ourselves (contrary to the exaggerated claims of a British press starved of any real meaty incidents to report). I am not saying that the English fans were all squeaky clean, but the Dutch and Germans were far worse, as witnessed by the largely unreported riot in Hamburg dealt with in the previous chapter. In fact the German police, and the German media, handled the English fans so well that by the third match in our group, we were allowed, and welcomed, anywhere. They knew we would behave because we had respect for them; they had treated us in a fit and proper manner. They had learned lessons from the England game there in 1986–7 and worked out an appropriate method of policing. Can you imagine anything like that happening over here?

No, in England we would be penned in up some back alley for hours on end with nothing to do and confronted by hordes of riot-equipped coppers. Just the situation to foster peace and harmony – if there's one thing that's sure to cheer you up, it's staring at a bloke who wants nothing better than to give you a legalised battering. We are not for one moment pretending that the police have an easy job of it – far from it – and we are certainly not attacking the police in general. Nevertheless they are doing a job which they chose to do, and one for which they are paid well, and by us. The average football fan is not a flying picket or a poll-tax rioter, he or she is an ordinary person with a job and a family who wants to spend an afternoon watching a game with thousands of like-minded football supporters.

Thanks to the Taylor Report, the football authorities have been dragged into the twentieth century and have started to treat us with respect by giving us stadiums fit to visit. Surely it is now time for the police to respond by softening their approach, especially towards the travelling fan. They've tried everything else, and nothing has really worked. Why not try something radical and be nice to people? We have a sneaky feeling that it might just work.

What follows is something we were told years ago by a gentleman who became a great friend of ours. For reasons too obvious to mention he is, and will always remain, anonymous.

The Filth

Back in the early seventies, I was a constable in the Metropolitan Police. As an East London boy, I was Hammers through and through. The chance to watch them for nothing every week was like a dream come true, but the other bonus was that a fight was guaranteed, and as a copper, you really couldn't lose, believe me. In those days, the Hammers didn't just have a serious crew, they had a serious crowd – almost everyone was up for it, and at every game something would happen which would involve us wading in, either with truncheons or with dogs, and we bloody loved it. For most of us it was a rare chance to get back at all the gits who made our lives a bloody misery day in and day out, and many's the time the lads on duty have taken out their frustrations on some poor bastard in the back of a van rather than drag him back to the nick and charge him.

Duty at Upton Park also gave me the chance to do my bit for the club, and I am proud to say that in all my days there I never nicked a Hammers fan. But I've certainly tugged a few of the visitors. I even had my picture in the paper once, leaping into the crowd during a disturbance. It's a great memento – I still have it.

The derby games were the worst of course, because we couldn't really tell if the supporters were Hammers fans or not. We're talking about the visitors' end, of course – Christ, no one was stupid enough to try it on at the home end, not in those days. They'd have been taken home in a carrier bag! At games like those, we had to sort out any trouble quickly. We just could not afford to let things go on for long as they had a habit of getting really out of hand.

I remember one game against Chelsea when things were really heavy. We had seized piles of weapons outside the ground but loads more had been sneaked in, and about halfway through the first half, a big fight broke out. There were boots and arms lashing out at anything that moved. We were told to get in and sort it out, but the general feeling was, 'Bollocks to that, get the alsatians in.' So the handlers went in with the dogs, but even they were getting a going over and we had to go in and get them out. The trouble was, the more of us who went in, the more the crowd turned on us, and for a time it really looked to be getting even more out of hand than usual. At times like those, it was just a case of grabbing anyone for an arrest – innocent or guilty, it didn't matter – and getting out as quickly as you could. That is exactly what I did, and I honestly think that the bloke I grabbed was as glad to be out of it as I was.

PART SEVEN
Solutions? What Solutions?

Chapter 16

Blowing Bubbles

SCUM, ANIMALS, THUGS, BIRCH 'EM, FLOG 'EM, LOCK 'EM UP, DEN OF SHAME, etc., etc., etc. The astute among you will already have recognised a few of the more popular headlines seen on the front of the British tabloid newspapers the day after any outbreak of trouble at a major game. However, while the media go to town on England supporters at every opportunity and hammer the fans of club sides who indulge in any sort of disorder (highlighting certain clubs in particular), it is a sad fact of life that we are living in a society which itself contains a great deal of violence. It is horrific to think that old folk being robbed and murdered in their own homes, women being kidnapped and raped, children being abused, muggings, road rage and so on are everyday facts of life in Britain, and terribly sad, too. Books, magazines, newspapers, television and computer games are also full of violence and while I would not be naïve enough to suggest that they have any effect on the average football supporter, we need to get some sort of perspective on what it is we are actually talking about here. There are problems running through the core of our society and football violence is just one of them: it is a relatively minor one, because as we have already said, it usually affects only like-minded individuals. While that does not make it right in any way, it is a lot less of a worry to us than someone abusing our children or robbing us in the street.

As we have discussed, the hysterical headlines so beloved of the press and the accompanying television coverage convince those citizens of this country who neither watch nor like football that the game and crowd violence go hand in hand. Anyone reading this book who has little interest in the game may well draw the same conclusion, and therefore we must now turn our attention to exploring what positive steps can be taken to try to relieve the problem. But is the scourge of crowd violence unique to football? Do other sports in England look at our game and shake their heads, murmuring incredulously, 'How can they put up with this?' or 'Nothing like that could ever happen here.'

A few months ago, the two of us were at a stadium when a fight broke out. The police came and questioned a few people before arresting one bloke, primarily because he was drunk and disorderly rather than for being involved in the fighting, which in fact he wasn't in any case. This caused a great deal of unrest among the crowd, who began hurling first abuse, then punches and finally rocks at the police officers, who quickly retreated to their vehicle to summon help. Within minutes, things were getting really out of hand. Some spectators were busy smashing up the police car as about three more cars, plus two vans with dogs and so on, arrived on the scene to drive back the crowd, who were by now attempting to rescue the arrested man from the clutches of the law. After about ten minutes the police managed to get this man into a van and took him away, closely followed by the rest of their colleagues, leaving the crowd to calm down on their own and the stadium staff to deal with it all, which actually they did very well.

This incident took place on a Sunday afternoon at a stadium in Essex which was staging a stock-car meeting. We mention it here merely to demonstrate that, despite what many people would have you believe, football is not the only sport that suffers from crowd violence. We have spoken to people who have been involved in trouble at ice hockey, basketball and speedway as well as cricket, boxing and rugby (both kinds). While it cannot be denied that the problem is greater in football, it must also be pointed out that many more people go to football matches than to other sporting events. So before we look in depth at what needs to be done to ease the problem, we need to make it clear that football is not alone. Other sports might bury their heads in the sand (or be relieved that their problems do not receive as much damaging publicity), but what we say here applies equally to the crowds they draw to their events, albeit on a smaller scale.

There is another point which needs to be taken on board, and that is that there are two significant types of violence among supporters – spontaneous and organised. The latter has been almost entirely solved at games, although this success has received far too little recognition. Throughout this book, we have looked at incidents involving fans from all over the country, and in most cases there is one common link: they are *group* activities. It is very rare indeed to see one-to-one fights at football for many reasons, the most important being that the vast majority of blokes are cowards and would not risk a confrontation they might possibly lose in front of their mates. The threat of arrest or ejection matters little – indeed, often it is seen as a badge of courage – but the chance of defeat, and for that defeat to be witnessed, is far too risky. It is also important to realise – and I am sure that most people will already know this – that you are far more likely to get a fat lip if you go to a nightclub on a Saturday night than you are if you go to a game on a Saturday afternoon. The nightclub environment tends to foster much more aggression among single males than football grounds, because of drink, drugs, women and so on, but here the violence is usually one-to-one, and therefore far more dangerous, as many policemen to whom we spoke were only too happy to confirm. But because it is small-scale, again it receives less publicity than football violence. However, we are concerned here with football, so let's look at what moves can now be made to improve safety even further.

Throughout this book we have included a great many verbatim accounts of incidents of crowd violence, but we have not even begun to scratch the surface. Anyone will be able to cite other major occurrences of trouble and if we wanted to be sensationalist towards this side of football, then this book would be the first in a series called *Great Rucks of Our Time*. But that is not what we are about at all. We have reproduced these stories to show that much of what happens at games (wherever it happens, it is linked to the game) is pre-planned and very well organised. However, it is clear that, thanks to the concerted efforts of clubs and supporters, the all-too-frequent pitched battles have been driven outside stadiums, almost certainly for good.

Yet pushing violence out of the stadiums themselves has driven it underground and forced it to become more organised. (If two rival gangs meet up some distance from the ground where their teams are playing, there must be more organisation involved than in a ruck in the stadium where the rivals are close together and can provoke each other on the spur of the moment.) This has enabled the establishment to claim great success in the battle against the hooligan, and while they have indeed won a significant victory, they have not won the war, as has been proven at Stamford Bridge and Dublin. It is therefore imperative that the game accepts that if trouble occurs which is linked in any way to any team, then it is a football problem. There are probably more organised groups of football supporters now than at any other time, and although not all of them are active in terms of violence, those that are tend to be very busy indeed. At the 1994–5 Auto Windscreens Shield final there was a great deal of trouble between Carlisle and Birmingham – not at Wembley, but in Southend-on-Sea! How can anybody with an ounce of sense discount this violence as anything other than football-related?

It is vital that the people within the game finally acknowledge that what they are dealing with is not simply crowd violence but basically gang warfare, involving people from all points of the social and economic compass of our society. As we have attempted to show, the average hooligan is a normal person like you, me, your son or your dad. They (we) do not have 'yob' tattooed on their foreheads, and away from the game they are usually normal human beings with normal lives. The persistent belief within football (and that includes some elements of the Football Supporters' Association) that the typical hooligan is a shaven-headed thug is one of the main reasons why the authorities have no real understanding of the problem.

This brings us to one of the key difficulties the FA face in their battle. As many people throughout the supporting world suspect, neither the clubs nor the FA particularly like supporters. If they could get away with it, you almost feel they would like to stage their games in grounds full of mums and dads (wearing suits, naturally) only until such time as they could finally hold them for the sole benefit of live television, which would save everyone involved a great deal of trouble as they would not have to deal with us at all. At the moment, they have to tolerate us because it is our money which keeps the vast majority of clubs afloat, but they do not have to like us, and they certainly do not have to talk to us.

At most games you go to, what do you talk about? If you're like us, you talk about the club: how crap they are (well, we are Watford supporters), which players are good, which are useless and what can be done to improve the team. You also talk about the game in general and if you go with a load of blokes, about the rucks which have gone off and, sometimes, what can be done to cure football violence.

If you run a business of any kind, one of the things you need to do is to carry out research among your customers and react to their feedback. The consumer is king: he or she dictates your marketing strategy and therefore your future growth. If you are really astute, you will find the people who are not using your product and talk to them to find out why not and act on that as well. Above all, you talk and listen to anyone and everyone and respond to what they tell you. Of course, if you do not, then sooner or later you will go under – it is as simple as that. However great your product, if no one wants it you will not sell it. Football has a problem; it has had one for many, many years and has worked hard to cure it. So far it has done a fairly reasonable job, but it is still failing to take the single step that will give it some of the solutions. Football has to talk to the very people it despises above all others; it simply has to talk to the people who take part in football violence, because they are the only ones who can tell you why they do what they do. If the FA bother to listen, they will be given all the answers they will ever need and they will be able to reduce the problem to the absolute minimum.

The clubs will tell you that they have regular meetings, or 'forums', to use the current buzzword, with the supporters' clubs in an attempt to explain decisions and to listen to the fans' views. But do they ever really listen? In any case, it would be foolish to assume that the minority of fans who cause the trouble actually join supporters' clubs – in most cases, such a move would not be considered in a million years. The fanzine and radio phone-in culture of the eighties and nineties has shown how spectacularly successful any platform for the views of the average supporter can become, but these hugely popular products are often condemned by the clubs for taking much-needed money away from the game. Clubs should recognise that they are a direct result of the distrust and frustration felt by supporters who still have little, if any, say in anything taking place at their club. In Italy, however, following the death of a supporter, the clubs took the initiative and contacted organised groups of hooligans such as the Ultras and the Irriducibili (literally, 'those who will not yield'), and talked to them about a solution to the violence. This actually had an effect in reducing the amount of fighting at the clubs. Would the board of Portsmouth ever consider speaking to the 6.57 Crew, or would Leicester City invite members of the Baby Squad to sit around a table with the board? Not until hell freezes over, because to do so they would have to accept that these groups had links with their clubs.

The establishment will, of course, go to great lengths to tell you that they have carried out their own studies and investigations into the problem for over twenty years, and indeed they have. However, the average supporter believes these inquiries have failed to come up with any reasonable or practical answers to the problem, despite the huge amounts of money spent on research (over £1 million by the Football Trust alone). The academics have merely succeeded in feeding an hysterical press with ever more outlandish theories to explain the behaviour of football supporters. (For example, one of the more off-the-wall offerings is that people involved in football-related violence have higher blood-sugar levels than 'normal' people because their lower-class diet contains an excess of junk food.)

What is painfully obvious to us is that the study of football hooliganism is one of the few growth areas in the employment of academics over the last twenty years. Like many supporters, we suspect that the jobs-for-the-boys syndrome is hard at work here. Some would even go as far as to say that their ineffectiveness is due in part to the need to justify and preserve their own jobs, and that therefore a cure would not actually be in their own interests. We are not academics, and nor would we wish to be, but from the research we have conducted for this book, and from our background of watching, and, yes, taking part in, football violence, we are convinced that we know as much as anyone about this problem. However, we do not for one moment imagine that the FA will be giving us a ring in the near future to ask our advice, although we would willingly give it.

Chapter 17

Where Do We Go From Here?

As supporters, we are convinced that violence among fans is one of only a number of difficulties affecting the game in this country, and, as we have said, in our opinion it is one of the minor ones. As far as we are concerned, clubs facing bankruptcy over a sum which would not buy a decent Second Division striker these days is a much more serious problem than a few blokes having a punch-up. Before we explore the options available to football, we need to repeat one thing, and that is that violence among fans will never be stopped completely, because some blokes just like, and some would say need, to fight. In any case, whenever you put between 10,000 and 30,000 people into a highly charged and emotive atmosphere, it is inevitable that sooner or later a conflict of some kind will take place and, sadly, it could well turn into a violent confrontation. So if you watch lots of games, sooner or later you will see someone throw a punch at somebody else. Happily, though, the higher numbers of police and stewards, with the help of CCTV, mean that the culprit will almost certainly be caught. The same can be said of the surrounding area on matchdays because the high-profile police presence does have a deterring effect on potential hooligans.

The real problems arise with the organised firms who, as we have shown, can arrive en masse anywhere and cause as much mayhem and disruption as possible. It is difficult to imagine how this issue can be dealt with, or even what steps could be taken to ensure that these groups do not travel or organise trouble. Yet something positive must be done. Banning offenders from clubs does not work, as most of the incidents occur during away games. Even when the culprits are caught, it is clear that the current community-service scheme most certainly does not work, either, because it is not enforced strictly enough and sentences are all too often ignored. (A friend of ours used to report to the station in the evening and tell the police that he had been unable to come during the afternoon because he had been at work. He was never found out.) Throughout our research, we failed to arrive at a single solution guaranteed to control the organised groups, despite conversations with many active members of mobs from all over the country, and that is very scary indeed.

It is not, after all, the FA, or the clubs, who have borne the brunt of this over the years, it is us, the fans. It is not the gentlemen of the FA who are herded around like cattle at away grounds, nor is it the staff of our club who have to watch their backs whenever they walk on to a railway platform on match-day. It is us, and we are sick of it; sick of looking over our shoulders and sick of that feeling you experience when you walk round a corner to face a group of young men from some other area of the country. Yet no matter what we say here, the general non-footballing public are convinced that the stadiums where our games are played resemble a Roman arena and that the average supporter matches the profile so often thrust before them, so let's look first at some of the common but ultimately outrageous and unworkable solutions offered before we deal with the reality. There are no easy answers, of course, and if solutions could be found to combat violence in our society as a whole, they would also solve the problem that affects our game. That is why we believe football-related violence can never be entirely eliminated; it does not, however, mean that nothing can be done to reduce still further this problem.

Following almost every off during the 1994–5 season, we sat

back at our breakfast tables and read about national service, longer sentences and corporal punishment, and during various conversations with people who have no link with football at all, these three 'solutions' have frequently been raised. As an ex-serviceman with over eighteen years' 'time in', Dougie has enough experience of the forces to know that they do not want national service foisted on them for a great many reasons, not least of which is the effect it would have on their reputation among other nations as highly professional volunteers. The introduction of any form of military service would make or (more likely) break any government which imposed it, whoever they were. But is it really a reasonable answer to the problem of football violence in any case? The role of the Services is to defend this country and, in doing so, they instil and nurture aggressive instincts in all serving personnel. There is no evidence to suggest that military service of any kind would have an effect on the amount of football violence we see in Britain and certainly, during my service career, young men from all three branches of the forces were among the worst elements of support at some clubs, particularly at matches taking place in Europe. The case for corporal punishment is even weaker, because fighting violence with violence is no answer at all, it merely provides society with the sense of revenge. It does not actually stop the fighting. What is almost certain is that neither of these 'solutions' will ever even be proposed until the government of the day has a desire to commit political suicide.

The case for longer sentencing for offending football supporters is far stronger, and in fact this already exists: if you commit an assault at a game you will receive a harder sentence than you would if you did the same thing anywhere else. This astonishes us, because we believe that if someone mugs an old lady it's a lot more serious than a ruck at a match. The courts don't always agree with that, however. On the subject of sentencing, in our opinion, the courts have got it completely wrong in this country. What is the point in fining or imprisoning someone for getting involved in trouble at football? If it can be proved that they went in search of trouble, used a weapon or carried out a vicious and premeditated attack, then fair enough, but we all know that in many cases, it's a spur-of-the-moment thing. Surely the best option would be to make more use of the community-service system and enforce it properly. That would at least serve some useful purpose. Compulsory community-service schemes have to be of more value than compulsory military service for young adults. Then again, we would have a great deal of time for anybody who provided things for young people to do in their spare time anyway. Isn't the lack of such opportunities another social problem which has a direct effect on the level of violence in our country?

The three 'solutions' outlined above are the responsibility of the government, and so individually, we have little influence over what happens there. Let's turn our attention to the schemes that various clubs have tried over the last few years to see if they have had any effect.

In the eighties, when trouble at games was widely reported and far more widespread, many clubs brought in identity cards and membership schemes. The government of the day, headed by Mrs Thatcher, even proposed a national ID scheme for a time. The club we refuse to name even banned away supporters for a period following the destruction of their ground by Millwall fans. All these measures were doomed to failure for one reason: money. (It is also worth noting their lack of effectiveness on another count: when Watford were in the lower divisions, if no visiting fans arrived at Vicarage Road, then the home supporters used to fight either the police or groups of Watford supporters from other towns, and I am sure that this was, and continues to be, repeated at other clubs all over the country.) You cannot impose restrictions on people entering your ground without suffering a loss of revenue, no matter how good your intentions, and very few clubs could ever hope to carry such a loss for long before going under. Banning away fans might be fine for Man United or Newcastle, because they have a big enough support base to fill the empty spaces (and wouldn't they secretly welcome that anyway?), but you ask the chairmen of Peterborough or Stockport for their opinions, and you can guess what the answer would be. Many clubs depend on that income, and without it they will fold quicker than an Italian striker in a penalty area.

Membership schemes and ID cards seem a great idea in principle, but in this case the concept was a poorly thought out knee-jerk reaction, and the compulsory imposition of them would, for many clubs, be financial suicide. That is why they will never happen. As the government is now considering a national identity card, along with all the attendant inherent risks and/or benefits (depending on your point of view), things may well change in the future, but we doubt it, because the schemes currently under consideration are all voluntary. Who in their right mind would take an ID card to a game where they might well get tugged?

If they had bothered to look, the clubs already had a significant weapon available in the battle against football violence but failed to consider the use of it for all games. The early kick-off is already a feature of local derbies. Many clubs bring the game forward to eleven o'clock to prevent fans drinking before the game in the hope that this will prevent trouble. In this instance it is not hugely effective because everyone is local and people just pile into the pubs after the game instead so things kick off later in the day. But early starts for other matches would reduce the number of travelling supporters and therefore opportunities for troublemaking, as well as policing costs and so on, which would benefit everybody in the long run. So why not bring all games forward to midday? In these days of live television dictating kick-off times (and even dates), what is so special about three o'clock on a Saturday afternoon?

Another tactic clubs regularly use is the all-ticket match. While this is a great idea in principle, it can cause more problems than it solves because most clubs impose stupid rules on supporters who want tickets, such as the dreaded voucher scheme at Watford. This encourages supporters to obtain tickets from anywhere they can, such as from touts, rather than queuing for tickets at inconvenient times. This then leads to the fans being located in the wrong place, creating the potential for further trouble. If I can buy a ticket on the day for a match that I know will end up being sold out, I will turn up early and go to the correct area of the ground where I can get a decent view. (We know that at many Premier League grounds this does not apply, but just bear with us.) But wouldn't that encourage visiting fans to go in the wrong end and cause mayhem? Well, yes, possibly it would, which is why the clubs and the police should get together and ensure that anyone caught causing any trouble in a part of the ground where he should not be is not merely ejected but arrested, held and charged with a criminal offence. He is only going to be in there to cause or incite trouble. I recognise that not everyone goes into the 'wrong' end in pursuit of violence and could be there as a result of a free ticket, or because they are there with someone who does support the other side. But in this context we are talking about blokes who go there looking for trouble. They are easily spotted because they swagger in and their eyes are everywhere. At the first incident of note, they are ready for action, adopting the classic chest forward, arms out pose so beloved of their type. I have no doubt that once people know they will face a certain court appearance rather than mere ejection, this ridiculous habit will cease overnight. (Just why do people persist in going into the wrong ends these days? You rarely see anyone getting away with it, just a few stupid idiots get slapped!)

More efficient and helpful (happy) stewards and policemen would be a vast improvement on the jobsworths we currently find ourselves saddled with. These people have a duty to deal with any complaints they receive – that is why they are there – and if you or I tell them that someone is using abusive or foul language or is an opposing supporter, then they must deal with it there and then. The current attitudes among these two groups do nothing but incite unrest. At present they are way out of touch. If you ever have the chance to go to the USA, you will see how people should be treated at sports events. It is an education.

The police, of course, have had a major influence on our game over the years and we have lived with the crap imposed on us as a result for so long that we take it without question. Why do we have to go straight into the ground when we get off the coach at an away game? Why do we have to be searched every time we enter the ground? Why do we have to travel to the club in midweek to get a ticket for the Shit Town game the following Saturday? These are all conditions stipulated by the police up and down the country which we readily accept, but they are not right.

Now that arrests and ejections at grounds are steadily falling, the time has come to scale down the involvement of the police inside our stadiums – and perhaps eventually to remove them altogether – and to use better stewarding. It does work; many clubs already use it with great success and it is time the rest followed suit. It is also important that the clubs, and football in general, realise that they have a duty to involve supporters in club business – as we are its paying customers, we have the right to be heard, and at every level. If that means employing a fans' representative within the club, so be it, but it has to be done and done soon, because the average fan will be a lot happier if he or she knows that there is a contact within the club who will listen to his or her views and that they will then be passed on to the staff.

There is also a role for the playing staff here. They are the focus of everything on matchday and have a duty to behave with dignity and pride. With the huge sums they earn comes a responsibility to the people who pay them – us. We do not want to know that our star player is looking to move on at the end of the season if we do not get promotion, nor do we want to hear that an international defender has had a punch-up outside a nightclub on a Friday night. It is a disgrace to see players refusing to complete transfers because the signing-on fee isn't high enough just as it is offensive for most fans to hear that the contract signed by almost any player who joins any club these days is not worth the paper it is written on. While we accept that any loyalty players profess to have is almost certainly superficial, we really do want to hear that players have been helping with young kids at a local school or have spent time talking to disabled groups – anything to boost the image of the club in the local community and the game which pays their wages. Of course, a great many players do a vast amount of work for charity and do not want it publicised, which is fair enough (and all power to them), but the clubs could glean a great deal of good PR for both themselves and the game by using their second-best assets to good effect.

On the positive side, many clubs have made fantastic strides to combat the problem of crowd violence and deserve praise for their efforts. Good luck to Leeds, Chelsea and others who are actually doing something about it all rather than sitting back and wringing their hands. Chelsea are a good example of a club who have at least experimented with some radical moves over the years, even if few of these made a big impact on the problem of football-related violence – remember electric fences, banning fans, tracking supporters to their homes and so on. It is widely accepted by anyone with any common sense that the use of CCTV has been the single most effective weapon ever devised in this battle, and that success has been acknowledged by the ever-expanding use of CCTV in town centres, which have themselves suffered far more from violent crime than most clubs put together.

Nowadays many clubs have brought in schemes to attract families back to the grounds, and we believe that youngsters should be actively encouraged to watch football, because in a few years they will turn into the sad fanatics that we already are. However, a word of caution before the clubs get too complacent: a lot of people who go to games these days – and we mean primarily men – are getting a little tired of not being able to vent their anger at the players performing in front of them because of the proximity of young ears. It is enough of a dampener to actually stop some people going. We go to football to release the tension and forget our troubles, after all. The clubs would do well to remember that it is the adults who pay the full price to watch games who fund them, not the under-tens. If they can provide areas for children and/or families, they should also designate enclosures specifically for adults, because that is what the customer wants.

Where Do We Go From Here?

On the subject of money, we are continually astounded at the prices charged to enter grounds these days. It is not just the Premier League which is at fault – in fact their clubs are not the worst. For those sides outside the top division whose attendances are falling – and there are many – isn't putting the prices up a daft thing to do? Isn't that the exact opposite of what retailers do? The clubs believe that the fans will continue to watch their teams whatever they charge us because we are a loyal group of obsessives and therefore have no choice whatsoever. Well, they are wrong – everyone has his limit, and sooner or later the clubs will realise that people will not pay the earth to go to a match when they can watch it on television or in the pub. Where will the inflated salaries and transfer fees come from then? Isn't it about time the clubs rewarded *our* loyalty?

We've had a look at the clubs and some of the things they might do to improve things, so let's turn our attention to the FA, the people who rule the roost. In this book we have been highly critical of the FA for a wide variety of reasons, the most important, and obvious, of which is that they are out of touch with the common supporter. The very first thing that the FA have to realise is that they cannot continue to ignore the views of the fans while they are still suffering such a serious problem of their own: there is no doubt that they are perceived by many as a governing body which is unfit to govern. In the case of the regulating bodies of most sports, their word is law, but in football things seem different.

A classic example was the Cantona affair. The FA should not have waited for Man United to impose a penalty on the player before acting; they should have announced a sentence of their own within a few days and that should have been the end of the matter. As it was, they waited to see what United would do and then decided on a further ban. This led to United saying they had been 'led to believe' that any sentence imposed by the club would be enough. This simply is not good enough. The decision-making process from Lancaster Gate has to be swift and absolute in all areas. As supporters, we need the FA to be resolute in all matters which involve the game, and we need strong personalities leading the battle. The current members, while good at what they do, are simply not forceful enough when dealing with the media, which is a great failing in a global sport. Consider, for example, the difference between Graham Taylor and Terry Venables. Both are fine managers but one is far better at handling the press than the other.

It is also clear that too many agents are becoming involved in football and that they have far too much influence for the good of the game. We have no problem with players having someone to represent their personal interests or wanting to earn as much as they can in their short careers, but we do have a problem with some oily little agent bleeding money out of the game to line his own pocket. It is surely only in the agent's interest if he plants a story, often with no substance, in the media saying that certain clubs are interested in 'his' player in the hope that he will receive an offer. Agents do have a valid place within football, but the FA have got to sort out a decent code of conduct for them, because at the moment, it seems that they have no control over them at all.

But we digress. So what positive steps can the FA take to improve the image of the game? We are not concerned with the product – that is perfect, and the game will continue to grow whatever rules are brought in to 'improve' things – but the image of football is crap. Within the game itself, the FA need seriously to enforce the rules already in existence. First they must move in hard on dissent. Snarling players and abusive managers have been an accepted, but not acceptable, part and parcel of our game for much too long, and they need to be stamped on quickly. The referees and linesmen are on the pitch to implement the rules the game has laid down, and while officials make mistakes, just as we all do, any sportsman must accept their decisions and get on with the game (and football can learn from cricket and rugby in this respect).

The 'gamesmanship' we often see is another provocative element that has begun to creep into the English game, and it is disliked by most fans. We know football is a man's game, most of us have played it before and we know that if you're tackled hard, you do not roll around like an epileptic (no disrespect intended), nor do you fly through the air with the greatest of ease if you are anywhere near the penalty spot. Officials should take swift and immediate action if these tactics are used, and that applies at all levels, be it the Premier League or the Rose and Crown Sunday Hackers' League. It is particularly important that these things are firmly dealt with, because – as we have said – the players' actions can have an effect on the crowd's behaviour. Controlling the players in this way will reduce football violence and improve the game's image. There is also a case for the FA to deduct points if teams exceed a set number of disciplinary points, something which, if implemented, would ensure that the management of a club took a very strict hold of their players' tempers. The often-levelled charge of 'bringing the game into disrepute' should be held up as the ultimate weapon against players letting down their clubs, the supporters and the game and it should be used to hammer those who seriously break the rules and/or the law. This would also help improve the standing of the game in general – too many players have got away with too much over the years with little more than a slap on the wrist, while agents sell their stories to the highest bidder. This is both wrong and harmful.

All of this may seem a little off the point, but it is relevant to us as supporters because what is seen as feeble leadership is alienating the fans who believe that football itself is being weakened as a result. It will not be tolerated for very much longer. Firm guidance is essential to our game; its effects will filter right through to us and a great deal of respect will be earned for the ruling body as a result. As it is, our game has already been sold down the river and no one has ever bothered to consult us at all.

It is all very well to pontificate about the generation of capital to fund growth, but at the end of the day the FA have damaged our game because the growth they talk about has not been forthcoming for many clubs. The FA are not the be-all and end-all – we are, and if we lose interest, the professional game will be lost and football will go back to council-owned playing fields.

Most supporters know the product inside out. Just because we are not professional players or coaches, it does not mean that we do not have valid ideas on ways to improve things, especially where they are relevant to our spectating environment. It should not have been left to the Taylor Report to secure for the spectators a decent level of comfort when watching the game. The FA and the clubs should have attended to that long ago – we told them often enough that it was what we wanted and needed.

Bodies like the Football Supporters' Association are all well and good, but do they actually achieve anything of any value? Does anybody at Lancaster Gate listen to what these people are saying? We doubt it. After the infamous Cantona incident and the subsequent events in Dublin, the FA did actually do something worthwhile: they set up the hooligan hotline, which is a great idea, and works well as far as we know. However, we can only guess as to its results, because they have not been well publicised; again, the FA have given themselves a golden opportunity, but have failed to take full advantage. Why don't the FA build on this by putting more responsibility on to us? We're grown-ups, we can take it. They already ask us to point out to the police supporters chanting racist abuse, so why not put the onus on us to alert them to people inciting or indulging in violence?

At present, if anything happens the law just steam in and arrest anybody who looks guilty, but it is rare for them to get the right person. Yet if we protest, we face arrest as well which usually means that the situation deteriorates. Why not get the stewards to come over and ask the people who saw an incident what happened and who did what? The stewards are familiar with almost every regular home supporter anyway, so why not make use of their knowledge? It might be risky, but it would certainly work, I am convinced. Why not mount an intensive anti-hooligan advertising campaign throughout the media? That would be effective and would also spread the word that the game is getting its act together. But we should not have to be saying this. Just what have they been doing all this time?

There are, of course, other groups who have influence over the way we are perceived, and two of those are the government and the media. Downing Street know full well that there is no political capital to be made from supporters through football because the vast majority of fans switch off from reality completely when they pass through a turnstile. Politicians can tell us as often as they like that they 'know where we are coming from', or that they have supported Chelsea or Sheffield Wednesday all their lives, but they are making a big mistake if they think that we give a toss. We know that they're not real supporters; they watch from executive boxes using their free season tickets and would not be seen dead driving back from God knows where on a Tuesday night. What is more, they know that we know.

The media are a different kettle of fish altogether. While we know that the things they write are crap, they have influence over the way people outside the game perceive us and that is very, very important. We have already looked at how the media have in the past both provoked trouble to create a story or blown up minor incidents to such an extent that they bear little resemblance to actual events. Although many people within the game are aware that these practices go on, nothing has ever been done to put a stop to this sordid exercise. This is crazy, because by allowing it, they are fostering the belief that the problem at football stadiums is massive, which it is not, as we have attempted to prove. The gentlemen (and ladies) of the press are in a powerful position and they have a duty to use that position for the good of the game which provides most of them with a very good living. They could start by promoting the positive things supporters have been doing to make things better for everybody. The decent fan's role in all of this has been largely forgotten by everybody.

At club level things are fairly straightforward, because, if nothing else, the FA and the clubs know that on a Saturday the behaviour pattern of fans will be almost totally dictated by the performances of the teams on the pitch or by a minority of supporters in the crowd. They also know that although they dissociate themselves from supporters outside grounds, the organised and travelling mobs will be indulging in all sorts of mischief in the name of their particular club and the game in general.

The search for a cure for violence among supporters at club level is one thing, but the national team, as we have seen, are another matter altogether. We have attempted to explain how the behaviour of a minority influenced by an even smaller minority can cause immense problems for anybody who wishes to watch England play, and of all the areas we have looked at, this is the one which gives us the greatest cause for concern. As we all know, in most cases all other loyalties are put aside for internationals because we are watching players who are representing our country and we, that is England, must not lose. That spirit is ingrained in the population of this country, irrespective of what the do-gooders say, and many supporters will carry that bullish pride into the crowd, where it can, on occasions, turn into a violent defence of the flag. That may be a bit of an extreme way of putting it, but there is no doubt that it sums it up. The influence of radical political parties on football supporters has also been examined elsewhere. So what is to be done? At home, the only real problem is a dislike of Wembley by most supporters, and in any case, no one other than the Scots have ever come to Wembley for a real pop. England away, however, is another question entirely.

To begin with, we have to make a statement that will seem dangerous, but we'll explain it afterwards, so don't throw the book across the room just yet. Forget Dublin. Yes, that's right, forget it. We know it was a terrible thing, and that it was without doubt one of the worst nights in the history of English football, but we must discount it because the events of that night were a one-off and will almost certainly never happen again with England (among other nations they almost certainly will, but that's another debate). Earlier in this book, I happily stated that I have not watched England play live since 1988 and I have watched very few of their games live on television, either, because the England team so rarely lives up to the potential of the talent that is available, nor does the side adopt the most effective tactics. Furthermore, I was sick and tired of being treated like a disease by the FA and looked upon by the media as nothing short of scum, and from what I hear and see, little has improved over the years.

So what has been done to address this problem since the early eighties, when things were really bad? Well, despite what the authorities say, very little, really. The only solid idea the FA could come up with was to make it as difficult as possible for supporters to get to matches abroad which, in a country with probably the largest travelling support of anywhere in the world, was quite a task. The formation of the England Travel Club, while a good idea in theory, served only to alienate the vast majority of fans who wanted to make their own way to a match to enjoy one of the greatest adventures supporters can have. The travel club might have imposed restrictions on the supply of tickets, but most supporters know that it is possible to get tickets at almost any game (in Dublin they were allegedly on sale outside the ground), and that independent travel, throughout Europe, especially, is fantastically easy. So what is the point of the travel club, other than to make it easier to track down anyone who gets himself caught up in someone else's trouble? While the FA made this token gesture towards ridding the national side of its apparently 100 per cent violent following, the police went intelligence-mental. At the merest hint of an England fixture, the Football Intelligence Unit switch into overdrive and send heaps of photographs and accompanying paperwork to whichever nation is unfortunate enough to be hosting us. This, together with our already tarnished image, obliges the police force of the host country to adopt a siege mentality, and before we know it, the British press is full of stories informing us that if any England supporter steps out of line, he will be deported.

This in turn leads the host police to view any England fan as a potential problem, and consequently all local police leave is cancelled, the riot gear is brought out and an aggressive stand is taken – just in case, of course. This aggressive and provocative policing encourages the very violence it is designed to prevent, and the press, once again, go to town with the cliché headlines and dubious photographs. The assumption that England fans started the trouble is obligatory and the fact that it has taken place abroad prompts the belief that everything revolves around racism, the old faithful chestnut in any debate about football supporters.

When England failed to qualify for the last World Cup, USA '94, the sigh of relief from the authorities in America could be heard from across the Atlantic, even though it was almost drowned out by the even louder sighs of relief at Lancaster Gate. Dougie was lucky enough to be in Florida during the early stages of the competition (although as Orlanda was home to the Irish, he avoided like the plague anything to do with football, for obvious reasons) and did some research into the plans that had been considered in the event that England qualified. The Americans had been shitting it at the thought that the England team would get through and that a few thousand supporters would join them. They had no real idea of what to expect (despite the fact that hundreds of thousands of English tourists visit America every year), and so they went way over the top, as the Americans can do.

For example, during the initial planning, the police had budgeted for an armoured personnel-carrier to be based in the city hosting the England team and its supporters, and the head of the World Cup security team (a Mr Ed Best!) was quoted as saying: 'I do not think we are overreacting.' While this in itself is pretty laughable, the fact that the FA and the police at home were involved in those plans shows once again what little regard these two organisations have for England supporters. The events of Dublin did England supporters no good at all in terms of public relations, but is interesting to note that the police, who dealt out some savage, and highly visible, beatings after that game, received very little in the way of condemnation from any quarter. Was it a case of 'a good thing, too', even though many people who were hurt were entirely innocent of anything other than attending the game?

Our suggestions to all involved in football as to what can be done to reduce football violence and improve the game's image are as follows. We must take the chance to tell the FA, the police and the government what action they can take to help us repair the image of England supporters abroad. Initially, you switch on the publicity machine and tell the world that the vast majority of English football supporters are decent, law-abiding people who have no time for football thuggery. They are not intent on destroying everything with which they come into contact, nor are they all fascist hooligans; all they want is to be able to support their team in safety and comfort. Next the authorities have to target the troublemakers and political extremists who see any England game abroad as an easy target for both recruitment and publicity. They should go to the foreign government and insist that steps are taken to ensure that any Englishman (or woman) arrested abroad in connection with football violence is charged and convicted in that country. It is also imperative that they serve their full sentence where the offence took place, because that would be a massive deterrent, as we have said. This would impose a financial burden on the host countries, who normally deport people en masse, but they should be able to recoup those costs from UEFA or FIFA, who make huge profits out of the game and have a duty to spend it on remedying something that is damaging football all over the world. This would of course have to be organised on an international basis so that it applied equally to all fans, not just the English but the Italians, Dutch and Germans.

As most of the games we are concerned with are played within the boundaries of the European Union, it should be made an offence under EC law to display at a football match any banner, other than the national flag, which shows any form of political message. In England's case, that action alone would put an end to the extremist-type symbols which are one of the main problems. It ought to be quite an easy ruling to achieve given the increasing influence of the EC these days, and we're sure such an initiative would be readily accepted by all member nations.

The British police must stop political extremists travelling to games (they know who they are, as they were only too happy to prove during the aftermath of the Dublin riot). While freedom of movement is one of the fundamental principles of the European Union, we think that allowing ordinary people to attend a football game in safety is far more important than the perceived rights of the odd convicted thug. It is also important that British policemen are allowed to travel openly with the England fans to every game, not only to monitor potential trouble, but also so that they can report back in our defence when the host country's supporters or police play up and the English fans wrongly get the blame. The police will say that they already stop anyone convicted of a football-related offence from travelling, but as the majority of hooligans are not on any police computer owing to the ejection-and-caution approach adopted over the years, this strategy is not as effective as it could be. This is something else that needs to be rectified for the good of the game in general as well as away internationals.

With the obvious exception of the known and convicted thugs, the FA should positively encourage supporters, both men and women, to go to England away games and spend time in the country in question and the tourism departments abroad should be encouraged to entice us into their cities to spend our money. During Euro '88, we (five geezers in a hire car) drove back from Frankfurt to Münchengladbach after the Russia farce using the back roads rather than the *autobahns*, and it was bloody fantastic. We stopped to rest and eat in small towns and villages and were welcomed with open arms by people who realised that we just wanted to visit their home towns rather than wreck them. Isn't that what it should be like for all of us? Other countries often welcome the Irish and the Scots, and that's the kind of reception we should be aiming to foster.

The key to all of this is one little word: respect. We are all too ready to acknowledge that respect is something which is earned, and over the years England supporters have not exactly been angels. Nobody who indulges in violence of any kind deserves consideration, but the genuine football supporters certainly do, and we should be getting it – not only from the FA, but from the police and the government. Respect and trust are great tools: treat people right and they will respond accordingly; treat them like shit and that is exactly how they will react. We've all seen enough over the years to know that.

Conclusion

The foregoing suggestions are, of course, merely our opinions, but we feel that they would have a positive effect on all fans in the drive to remove the disease of violence from our game. We are not naïve enough to presume that the introduction of these simple changes would make football violence vanish overnight. Besides, as we have made clear, we firmly believe that it will never leave us completely. It is still regarded as fashionable among young men to fight at football, just as it is looked upon as a status symbol to be part of an organised mob or to support a club with a reputation for violent fans. Getting drunk, fighting and causing mischief are for many part and parcel of growing up. People might not like it, but they have to accept it as the truth and as one of the fundamental reasons behind the problem. Violence among supporters became linked to football because it is the most popular sport in the world and its male-dominated environment provides the perfect breeding ground for what the academics would call a tribal atmosphere, with its own rituals, code and honour. The defence of a reputation and pride in your own club are all part of this culture and offer something that many young men need: the chance to prove themselves and to make the transition from boy to man.

Earlier on in this book, we explained how it was that we became involved in violence of this kind, so perhaps we should explain how it was that we stopped because it may give you an insight into our way of thinking and provide an example of sorts. We make no apologies for saying this, but when we were up for it, we had a bloody great time and far too many laughs to mention here. However, after a few seasons, things started to change as the nucleus of the mob we were running with started to fall apart due to pressure of work and family commitments. On top of this, the use of weapons seemed to become more and more widespread and things started to get far too heavy and violent. There are only so many times you can have a blade pulled on you before it starts to become a worry. It was certainly starting to become far too regular for our liking!

There were other factors of course. Living where we do, in a London overspill town, we are surrounded by Spurs, Arsenal and Chelsea fans, as well as hordes of Hornets, and on occasions this club rivalry was carried over into our social life because people knew that we had been, on occasions, active with our club.

The final straw, however, was one particular incident where the two of us took a serious hiding which left us both with broken bones – Eddy had a fractured skull and Dougie had two broken ribs. On the drive home, we took a long hard look at what it was we were actually doing, realised that it just wasn't worth the hassle any more, and so we both got out. But we did this because we wanted to, not because of any outside influences or pressure. We just got bored of it, simple as that. I am sure that many people reading this will have experienced that same feeling, although football has never been quite the same.

Football is the people's game. It attracts millions of supporters from all walks of life and is wholly dependent on those supporters for its survival. For the vast majority of people who watch the game, it is a perfectly safe, enjoyable activity, and long may it remain so. But the sheer excitement and passion generated by the game make it inevitable that within those numbers there will be individuals who are, or have the potential to be, confrontational. During all our conversations and meetings with supporters from clubs at all

Conclusion

levels throughout England, it became clear that a great many supporters believe that football violence is here to stay in some form or other, and you know that we both share that opinion. It may not be the perfect ending you wanted (depending on your personal point of view), but it sure as shit is the truth, and time will prove it to be so.

This book would not have been
possible without the help of football supporters
from all over the country.

If you have any views on the contents of this
book or would like to help us with our football-
related research please do not hesitate to
contact us at the address below.
We will add your name to our database
and send you regular questionnaires on
the issues that affect *you*, the
football supporter.

This is an opportunity to have your say.

All correspondence will be treated with the
utmost confidentiality.

Please write to:
Fandom
P.O. Box 766, Hemel Hempstead, Herts,
HP1 2TU.

If you have enjoyed *Everywhere We Go*, you may enjoy the following special edition Headline Review non-fiction 20/20 titles also available from your bookshop or *direct from the publisher*.

FREE P&P AND UK DELIVERY
(Overseas and Ireland £3.50 per book)

Psycho	Stuart Pearce	£4.99
Left Foot Forward	Garry Nelson	£4.99
The Kindness of Strangers	Kate Adie	£4.99
The Floating Brothel	Siân Rees	£4.99
The Man Who Ate Everything	Jeffrey Steingarten	£4.99

TO ORDER SIMPLY CALL THIS NUMBER

01235 400 414

or visit our website: www.madaboutbooks.com

Prices and availability subject to change without notice.